Healing Into Action

A Leadership Guide for Creating Diverse Communities

Cherie R. Brown & George J. Mazza

National Coalition Building Institute (NCBI)
1120 Connecticut Avenue, Suite 450
Washington, D.C. 20036
(202) 785-9400

HEALING INTO ACTION
A LEADERSHIP GUIDE FOR CREATING DIVERSE COMMUNITIES

Copyright © 1997 National Coalition Building Institute (NCBI)

ISBN 0-9659731-0-7

Library of Congress Catalogue Card Number 97-92381

Typesetting and Printing by Nighthawk Communications
Illustrations by James Graham

National Coalition Building Institute (NCBI)
1120 Connecticut, N.W, Suite 450, Washington, D.C. 20036

To contact NCBI call (202) 785-9400

Special Thanks

To the people at the W. K. Kellogg Foundation, who made the
publication and dissemination of this book possible

Acknowledgments

I want to acknowledge a few of the many people who have contributed to the publication of this work. Much of the theory and examples in *Healing into Action: A Leadership Guide for Creating Diverse Communities* I developed through directing the National Coalition Building Institute (NCBI) since its founding in 1984. The *Guide* is also the result of the efforts of dozens of NCBI leaders who have worked with thousands of people throughout the world, testing and retesting NCBI principles in diverse cultures and environments. The NCBI leaders have a fierce commitment to learn the best ways to end oppression, and they have worked hard on this project, often under demanding circumstances and for little or no financial reward.

I want to thank my colleague, George Mazza, who collaborated with me in putting on paper what we have learned at NCBI. I appreciate his tireless efforts to put our years of work into a simple, readable form.

Since the Guide grew out of the work of the Leadership for Diversity Initiative (LDI), I want to acknowledge the NCBI chapter directors and leaders who headed the LDI teams in their respective cities: Peg Lewis, Guillermo Lopez, and Phyllis Alexander in Allentown, Pennsylvania; Caryn Corenblum and Smith Williams in Birmingham, Alabama; Collin Rustin in Durham/Chapel Hill, North Carolina; and Larry Bell and Dvora Slavin in Washington, District of Columbia. Their commitment to end racism, coupled with their hard work to improve the quality of life in their communities, inspired the writing of this manual.

I want to acknowledge Harvey Jackins, founder of Re-Evaluation Counseling, who has spent a lifetime building a theory and practice of healing and liberation, which became an integral part of the work of the LDI teams. Many of the principles in this manual are derived from Re-Evaluation Counseling.

I want to acknowledge the invaluable contributions of Alvin Herring, the Chief Operating Director of NCBI, who was my partner every step of the way in directing LDI. From its inception, Al's ceaseless efforts guaranteed the success of LDI. His love and commitment sustained me and the LDI directors over the three-year project. When it came to writing this manual, his comments and suggested examples were often the ones we used.

I want to thank Anne Streeter, NCBI's Business Manager, who deftly performed all of the countless tasks that allowed us to coordinate four major programs in four cities simultaneously. Anne's lifetime commitment to fighting racism was evident in all of her work on behalf of the project. In the process, Anne also did a great deal to assist the local Washington efforts of LDI.

Finally, I want to acknowledge Betty Overton, NCBFs project advisor at the W. K. Kellogg Foundation. She believed in the work of NCBI from the very beginning and has continued to be a great friend and ally.

C.R.B.

What People Are Saying About *Healing Into Action*

"Healing Into Action is a book that believes in progress obtained by non accusatory action and truly makes people see another group's perspective. It's very practically organized to be used for training and to stimulate participation."

—FRED CIPOREN
GROUP VICE PRESIDENT AND PUBLISHER
PUBLISHERS WEEKLY

"As we move into the 21st century, guide books such as *Healing Into Action* offer new insights and new principles around which we can organize our work and express our commitment to represent all of the people. The National Coalition Building Institute has made great strides in our islands toward building bridges between our diverse and multicultural peoples and in reducing prejudice and bigotry. NCBI has helped lead the way in our state in modeling what it truly means to create a caring and open community."

—THE HONORABLE BENJAMIN J. CAYETANO
GOVERNOR OF HAWAI'I

"As a member of Congress who must build bridges daily with local constituents and national leaders, I find *Healing into Action* an essential resource. NCBI has put together in one manual key skills that every elected official needs."

—CONGRESSWOMAN LOUISE SLAUGHTER
NEW YORK

"*Healing into Action: A Leadership Guide for Creating Diverse Communities* provides an inspirational vision of what's possible for our communities: working together effectively through viewing our differences as resources rather than as problems. NCBI's model works, and it does so because it's founded in profound respect for the hurts people have experienced and for their capacity for courage when they take on changing the world one heart at a time.

"This Guide is extremely useful and practical. For each leadership principle, there is a theoretical explanation, a specific example of the principle from NCBI's vast experience of conducting workshops around the world, and an activity to bring forth the principle in your life. If you have participated in one of NCBI's workshops, the Guide is a great reminder of the power of the healing you saw at work (and a great incentive to keep it alive). If you have not participated in a workshop, you can use this book to start your own journey."

—ALAN B. TEASLEY, PH.D
EXECUTIVE DIRECTOR FOR GRANTS ADMINISTRATION
DURHAM (NC) PUBLIC SCHOOLS

"Healing Into Action is an especially beneficial resource. For those of us seeking insightful guidance and effective strategies in inter-religious, inter-ethnic dialogue, this book will be invaluable. Community activists, civic leaders, political leaders and those in the religious community will turn to this book repeatedly. It is simply superb."

—RABBI DAVID SAPERSTEIN
DIRECTOR
RELIGIOUS ACTION CENTER OF REFORM JUDAISM

"Our Union reflects the faces of an increasingly diverse workforce through its membership. The NCBI programs presented at our conferences at various levels have been extremely beneficial. *Healing Into Action* is an important resource for Unions in our efforts to build an inclusive labor movement for economic and social justice in communities where workers of diverse backgrounds live. In setting aside cultural differences, all workers can collectively unite around important workplace issues that affect them and their families."

—GEORGE BECKER
INTERNATIONAL PRESIDENT
UNITED STEELWORKERS OF AMERICA

"NCBI's work with PBS staff has provided us with powerful tools for genuine dialogue. Their positive approach has helped us build relationships across PBS and given us a renewed sense of community in our workplace. Anyone interested in understanding and communicating the value of diversity will benefit from *Healing Into Action.*"

—CAROLE DICKERT-SCHERR
VICE PRESIDENT, HUMAN RESOURCES
PUBLIC BROADCASTING SERVICE (PBS)

"We have been using the NCBI program and principles outlined in their new guide for the past two years with our local union leaders and activists. The NCBI principles are clear, straightforward and have helped us generate trust among our elected leaders and staff and create greater understanding of our responsibility to include everyone!"

—DANNY DONOHUE
PRESIDENT
CSEA LOCAL 1000, AFSCME

Table of Contents

Introduction

The National Coalition Building Institute (NCBI), founded by Cherie R. Brown, is an international, non-profit leadership development organization that assists a broad range of organizations in creating more inclusive environments. Since its founding in 1984, NCBI has grown into more than 40 city-based chapters and 30 organizational affiliates in the United States, Canada, England, Germany, and Switzerland. NCBI has worked with tens of thousands of people, training a new generation of leaders who can welcome diversity. NCBI has worked with federal, state, and local governments; labor unions; elected officials; corporations; trade associations; universities; community groups; congregations; public schools; foundations; police and fire departments; prisons; and coalitions of community activists.

From 1993 to 1997, NCBI, with the assistance of the W. K. Kellogg Foundation, launched the Leadership for Diversity Initiative (LDI), an intensive, targeted training program for civic leaders in four U.S. cities: Allentown, Pennsylvania; Birmingham, Alabama; Durham/Chapel Hill, North Carolina; and Washington, District of Columbia. The goal of the project was to provide community leaders with the essential skills that could enable them to become effective resources for fostering diversity, not only within their own organizations, but also within the broader community.

Healing into Action: A Leadership Guide for Creating Diverse Communities grew out of the success of LDI. NCBI has learned a great deal about empowering leaders for diverse communities. The Guide provides a simple, practical, skill-oriented handbook for busy community leaders who are looking for help in taking leadership in increasingly diverse environments. In our writing, we had in mind such people as chiefs of police, superintendents of schools, students, teachers, labor activists, grassroots community organizers, religious leaders, business managers, and any other person who exercises community leadership.

Consistent with our intent to assist busy leaders, we have distilled NCBI's collective wisdom into concise leadership principles. Each principle is illustrated with theory, a related example, and an activity that can assist the reader in developing the skills required to put the principle into practice.

We have organized the book by arranging the leadership principles into four broad categories. In the first section, Building Environments to Welcome Diversity, we provide the nuts and bolts of creating structures and establishing practices that support leaders who are committed to creating more inclusive communities. In the second section, Healing Ourselves to Change the World, we emphasize that to become an effective leader, we have to tend to our own healing. To become a leader in a diverse community, we have to take stock of the misinformation we have about various groups, and we have to recognize how our own personal histories may distort our ability to think creatively in the present. In the third section, Becoming Effective Allies, we focus on the skills needed to build better relationships across group lines. We have included information on the art of conflict resolution, which relies on the fundamental skill of listening to people with whom we disagree. In the fourth section, Empowering Leaders to Lead, we present skills that sustain leaders. Leaders must be free to take individual initiative, to give and receive support, and to handle attacks effectively.

At the end of each of the four sections, we have provided a story that demonstrates how the principles operate in concert. These four stories, which we have called Principles in Action, show how each of the NCBI chapters in the four LDI project cities used the principles in the preceding section to create more inclusive communities.

We envision many possible uses for the Guide. Organizations may use it as a workbook, discussing one principle at a time at regularly scheduled meetings as a form of continuing diversity education. Leaders who are confronting a difficult problem might use the *Guide* as a checklist, considering whether they may have overlooked one of the principles in analyzing the situation confronting them. For those who have already attended an NCBI training program, the Guide may serve as a refresher manual, reinforcing the lessons of the training sessions. However the Guide is used, we have intended that people will not just read the text but put it into practice.

If this handbook is your first encounter with NCBI, you can acquire additional training through NCBI's international training institutes, as well as through other training programs that NCBI offers in countless organizations and communities around the world throughout the year.

At NCBI we are pragmatic. We are interested in what works. We wrote this Guide to help leaders who want to be effective. We are constantly learning and passing on new information. If you find this booklet helpful in dealing with a particular issue, let us know. We enjoyed the task of presenting NCBI principles in a short, practical guide, and we welcome your comments and letters.

C.R.B./G.J.M.
June 1, 1997
Washington, District o f Columbia

Building
Environments

to Welcome
Diversity

1

Principle: **guilt** *is the glue that holds prejudice in* **place.**

Theory:

Many diversity training programs rely on guilt to motivate people to change their prejudicial attitudes. The sessions often consist of moralizing or blaming people for their privileged positions. Some programs review all of the ways in which participants have been racist or sexist or acted in other oppressive ways. These common approaches do not work. Condemning people, shaming them, and making them feel guilty are all unproductive strategies: They increase defensiveness rather than creating an opening for change. Guilt is especially useless, because it thrives on our turning inward, focusing on our own bad feelings about ourselves, rather than directing our energies outward, toward the work of becoming an ally. People change more readily when they are lifted up and appreciated, not when they are made to feel guilty.

Example:

A large metropolitan police department was under increasing public scrutiny for alleged racist practices. Daily articles attacking the department appeared in both local and national newspapers. Recent high profile trials produced evidence indicating widespread racism in the department. With the increased media attention, the police officers became more defensive and isolated. When the police commission decided to introduce diversity training for officers in the department, the officers saw the training as one more attack on the department. The more community groups pointed out the police department's failings, the less the officers were willing to hear the criticism. They resisted all suggestions for change by saying, "We're the best police department in the world." With the adoption of this siege mentality, the officers could not honestly look at the racism in the police force.

Activity:

Think of someone you work with or in your community whose prejudicial behavior you've tried to change. How many times have you tried to correct that person's behavior and it didn't work? Condemning people rarely helps them to change their behavior. Instead, think about what you honestly appreciate about the person. Also consider the ways that person has made any progress, even if it's only slight, on the issue that is of concern to you. Practice telling that person the things she is doing right. Appreciation leads to action; condemnation leads to paralysis.

People are often afraid to appreciate someone whose behavior they disapprove of for fear that the appreciation will keep the oppressive behavior unchallenged. However, only by seeing what is human in the person who acts oppressively can we hope to bring about change. All of us are more receptive to suggestions to change when we know we are liked.

Principle:
welcoming

diversity means every person counts

and every issue counts

Theory:

Workplaces and educational institutions need to be particularly sensitive to creating environments that welcome women and people of color. It is also important to remember that every person is important, even those who belong to majority groups that have historically oppressed other groups. For example, if White men end up feeling that their concerns are insignificant, they may react with a backlash. Then, the ultimate goal of creating a healthy environment that values diversity is undermined. We need to communicate that every person is valued and that every person's issue counts.

Example:

At a Southwestern U.S. university, ugly racist flyers that targeted Latino students were being circulated on campus. To respond to the incident, the university president invited NCBI to lead a day-long assembly for all students in a huge auditorium. At one point in the workshop, we were trying to demonstrate that one of the ways to end the targeting of others is to heal the places where we feel shame about ourselves. We also wanted the group to understand that we need to listen to every group, even ones that have historically oppressed other groups. We brought up in front of the assembly a White male student who said he was ashamed of being White and male. We encouraged him to heal the shame by leaping into the air and shouting, "It's great to be a White man!" While he was leaping, we asked the rest of the students to applaud him. The next day the dean of the campus called and told us she was pretty sure she knew who had been passing around the ugly racist flyers. The student came to her office and said, "If White men can also get applauded in diversity work, then I want to learn how to be part of leading prejudice reduction workshops here on campus."

We can, and hopefully will, end all racism, and there will still be people with different skin colors. We can, and hopefully will, end all sexism, and there will still be males and females. When we communicate that there is nothing inherent in being male or White that leads to oppressive behavior, we enable members of these groups to take an honest look at the societal conditioning that leads to oppressive thoughts and actions. Reclaiming pride prepares people to face their discriminatory patterns.

Activity:

Consider the various ways you identify yourself (e.g., First Nation/Native American, African heritage, European, male, Lutheran, bisexual, owning class, overweight, divorced, Canadian, etc.). Is there a part of your identity of which you are not proud? Is there a part of who you are that you tend to hide from people? One of the most profound blows to oppression is claiming legitimate delight in who we are. You may want to experiment with this new point of view by trying the phrase, "It's great to be _____!" Notice where you struggle in claiming pride in who you are. This is the preliminary work that must be done to work against all forms of oppression.

Reclaiming pride in our identities entails knowing our histories, becoming familiar not only with the side of history that causes us shame but also with the side that offers us hope. Ever mindful not to distort historical realities, it is nonetheless possible, even in the midst of the worst acts of oppression, to claim as our ancestors the few people who resisted the oppression. For example, in the present, it is useful for many people of

German heritage to remember that there were heroic Germans who resisted Nazi anti-Semitism. There were German aristocrats, politicians, clergy, and university students who risked their lives in opposition to Hitler. Along with the unfathomable devastation of the Holocaust, this minority tradition of resistance is also part of the history of the German people. By aligning themselves with the historical resistance movement, present-day Germans who struggle with claiming pride in their heritage may find a way to recover who they are. The same process is available to many other groups. Southerners may need to know the history of Southern abolitionists; men may need to discover the history of leading male feminists. When people are left only with shame, especially following horrendous histories of oppression, we abandon them to the shame, and then they are more susceptible to repeating the cycle of oppression.

When we can model that every person counts and every issue counts, there will be less need for the type of backlash that undermines the efforts to achieve diversity. For example, people who speak out so ardently against affirmative action for disenfranchised groups, even when they are wrong, are often simply trying to say, "Don't leave me out-don't forget about my group!" When we take the time to listen to all voices, including these, we will be able to build even stronger intergroup coalitions.

HEALING INTO ACTION

Notes

Is there any part of who you are of which you are not completely proud? For your own benefit, you may want to make a short list.

_____

_____

_____

_____

_____

_____

_____

Using the list you just made, practice reclaiming pride. "It's great to be _____!"

_____

_____

_____

_____

There may be somethings about ourselves that we rightfully resist calling great. For example, people with histories of sexual abuse would never say there was anything great in being abused. To reclaim power, they might be encouraged to say it's great to be a survivor.

Principle:
treating
everyone the same may be

unintentionally oppressive

Theory:

A common response to diversity programs is, "Why are we always focusing on group differences-wouldn't it be better if we stopped talking about all these groups and simply treated everyone as a unique human being?" Although it is an important goal to treat each person as a unique individual, it is also important to remember that many people have been mistreated, not simply as individuals but as members of a group. When we ignore the particular ways in which groups have been oppressed historically, we may end up failing to see the important needs of individuals in that group.

Example:

Two colleagues, Barbara, an African American woman, and Connie, a White woman, were on a business trip together. After a day of meetings, they decided to have dinner together at the small country inn where they were staying. Barbara had invited a male colleague, who was also African American, to join her and Connie for dessert. While the dinner dishes were being cleared away, Barbara kept nervously rushing out to the lobby to check to see if her friend had arrived. After the third time, Connie said, "Hey, relax! This is a small inn. He'll find us. What's going on?" Barbara responded, "I can't just relax. Black men always get stopped in hotel lobbies, especially small ones like this one, because the hotel staff often automatically assume that a Black man couldn't possibly have any business in a place like this. I want to make sure he gets treated right." By thinking that her Black colleague had the same experiences she had, and responding to her in the same way she would to a White colleague, Connie failed to see how Barbara was still having to handle racism.

Activity:

At work or in your neighborhood, practice asking people who belong to groups other than your own how they may continue to experience discrimination. We may be embarrassed to ask, thinking that by just asking such questions we're demonstrating how uninformed we are. The opposite is actually true. There is no way we can know about the experiences of others without asking. There was no way that Connie would know why her friend was pacing the lobby without her asking. Imagine what workplaces could be like if we were open to asking and then listening to how our colleagues experienced mistreatment as members of particular groups.

We could transform our workplaces if people genuinely had a sense that their colleagues and supervisors wanted to know about their experiences at work. Asking these questions-not just once but on a regular basis-can give any worker, supervisor, or leader useful new information on which to base decisions.

Principle:
meetings
go better when everyone is
included.

Theory:

Building an environment that welcomes diversity requires gaining the active participation of all the people in the community. We can easily overlook the fact that most meetings favor people who are articulate and willing to speak in public. Many of us may not only find it difficult to speak in public, we may also struggle with figuring out what our opinions are. Members of certain groups may struggle with these issues more than others. Women, people of color, young people, working class people, immigrants, people with disabilities, and elders have often been told either they can't think or what they think is unimportant. As a result, it is not surprising that members of these groups often find it hard to put forward their thinking in mixed groups, especially when the discussion is being formed by others. Without attention to the ways in which membership in particular groups affects who speaks and who is silent, many key voices go unheard.

Example:

A number of women from the United States who attended the United Nation's Women's Conference in China in 1995 noticed that women from developing countries would not readily speak in the sessions, while women from Western countries always had plenty to say. Even when the session moderator would specifically encourage women from non-western countries to contribute, U.S. women would quickly jump in and dominate the discussion. Eventually, moderators who were attentive to this dynamic had to set ground rules that encouraged the participation of the whole group.

Activity:

Here are three ways to encourage greater participation at group meetings:

Set Up Pairs. When a topic is up for discussion, ask the entire group to form pairs. Within the pairs, each person takes a set amount of time to think out loud. Without comment, one person simply listens attentively to the other person. Most people find this process helpful in formulating and articulating an opinion. Once the group reconvenes, everyone already has a point of view to contribute.

Establish Ground Rules. To encourage the participation of all people in a group discussion, it may be useful to set ground rules. For example, you might establish the rule that no one speaks a second time before everyone first has a chance to speak. Depending on the composition of the group, you might also establish an express speaking order. For example, you might say, "First, let's hear from women; next, let's hear from people of color; next, let's hear from working class people."

Encourage people to stretch themselves. Ask people to set personal goals regarding how they plan to behave in a group. For those who tend to dominate discussions, ask them to stretch in trying to listen and encourage the participation of others. For those who tend to become invisible in groups, ask them to stretch in trying to volunteer responses to every question. You might try setting up a "buddy" system, where two people agree to support each other in carrying out their individual goals.

The more people are involved in the process of any undertaking, the more ownership they will take in the results.

Principle:

recognize

and work with the diversity already present in what appear to be homogenous groups.

Theory:

In trying to combat racism and other forms of oppression, many people become discouraged when they are unable to create a diverse group. Instead of giving in to the frustration, the first step is to work with the diversity already present in the group that exists. Even in the most homogenous group, there are inevitably significant differences that go unnoticed. In addition to race and sex, the work on diversity includes age, religion, disability, socio-economic class, sexual orientation, ethnicity, marital status, parenting status, profession, as well as many other differences. Taking the time to examine these and other issues can be invaluable, not only for creating a climate that welcomes the differences already present in the group, but also for laying the groundwork for becoming more inclusive of other differences. When people can notice and appreciate diversity within their own groups, they learn the skills that help them become more open to other forms of diversity, including race and sex.

Example:

At a bank in a Southern U.S. city, the organizer of a diversity training program became distraught because the participants were all White, middle class Christian men. She wondered how they could learn to handle diversity more effectively in such a homogeneous group. We responded that we would gladly lead the workshop and work with the diversity we had in the room. During the session, the participants were surprised to realize how much diversity existed among them. There were major differences in terms of age, religion, marital status, parenting, health issues, military experience, and socio-economic class background. By focusing on the diversity in what initially appeared to be a homogeneous group, we helped them notice all the different aspects of diversity. As a result, they were better prepared to welcome women and people of color. At the next training session, the demographics of the group changed. Twenty percent of those who were present were people of color.

Activity:

Think about the people at your work, your place of worship, or in your neighborhood. Ask yourself what diverse groups do they represent. In particular, what are the differences in terms of sex, race, age, religion, class, ethnicity, profession, place of birth, sexual orientation, marital and family status, and disability? Are there additional differences that are significant?

By focusing on every aspect of diversity, we can train ourselves to remember that every group counts. We must create lives that are big enough to welcome every group and every issue. The more we accept that the people around us don't have to be just like us for the world to be safe, the more we will seek out people from completely different cultures and world views.

Principle:

people

can take on tough issues more readily when the issues are presented in a spirit of hope.

Theory:

All too often, we are bombarded with stories of doom and gloom: The world is heading to destruction, and though there's little we can do about it, we have to try anyway. When we mobilize people to action by communicating hopelessness and despair, we tend to get two kinds of responses. First, some people will join us, sharing our sense of panic or desperation. Such people are often trying to respond to the present situation out of grief or anxiety connected to the past. When people are acting on the basis of painful emotion, they are too upset to think well. Second, other people may hear the message and close their hearts and their doors-it may be just too difficult to pay attention when the depressing message triggers feelings of insignificance and powerlessness.

It is far more effective to call people to action on the basis of hope. How much more willing we are to respond when we hear, "You're just the group to do something about this" or "We can make a difference" or "We're on the threshold of turning around racism in this country, and you're just the folks to take the lead!"

Example:

The chief of police in a major metropolitan area found the racial divisions within his police department disturbing. He tried to shift the tone in the department, but the more ominous warnings he issued, the more the racial climate deteriorated. He had nearly given up hope of moving things forward. When his officers responded positively to a program led by two NCBI facilitators, he was shocked. What was different in the NCBI presentation was its tone. The NCBI trainers never blamed the officers. The trainers neither condemned the police nor portrayed the police department's situation as hopeless. Instead, they showed genuine respect for the officers' commitment to public service. The trainers communicated an upbeat, hopeful message that freed the officers to look at their racism.

Activity:

When soliciting support for any project, whether it's a simple administrative task in an organization or a community-wide initiative, use confident, upbeat language that inspires people to do their best. You may want to incorporate some of the following phrases in recruiting support:

> *"It's clear that we all care deeply about this issue."*
> *"I know that you're eager to figure out how to be an ally."*
> *"We have a wonderful challenge at hand. There's no reason that we can't do something about this."*
> *We like to take on tough things around here. It challenges us to be creative."*
> *"What a wonderful opportunity we have to try out some new things."*

People can accomplish a great deal when they are convinced that their efforts can make a difference.

Principle:

building

a team around us is the most

powerful way to bring about

institutional change.

Theory:

NCBI used to lead diversity training programs in community organizations and on college campuses with the expectation that the work would carry on long after we were gone. Within a year after our training programs, we often noticed that the work had stopped. We discovered that most individuals could not sustain the commitment to take on institutional change. They experienced the work as being too hard and they became discouraged. By experimenting, we learned that by establishing core teams, made up of people who were committed not only to the work but also to each other, the diversity training work continued year after year. The people on the local teams grew to became intimate friends, sticking by each other often in hard times, moving forward in spite of any setbacks. To succeed, every leader needs the support of a team.

Example:

Several college students on a campus located near a Native American reservation in the Western part of the United States were concerned about the lack of support for the Native peoples in the region. They tried to bring programs to their campus on Native issues but failed to get community support. One of the students learned through NCBI that to be effective she had to build a team around her. She convened 20 students and asked them to support her, to help her work through her fears in taking action. They met together in a weekly support group, each taking a turn to look at the fears that got in the way of taking the next step. The students decided that they would be as committed to each other as they were to the work they were doing in the community. They also did fun things together, socializing and hanging out. Then, as a team, they went to a city council meeting to protest the treatment of Native peoples in their community. They were such a powerful, organized presence that over time the city council established several new policies favorably affecting Native Americans in the community, including a resolution to establish a local holiday in honor of Native Americans. The preliminary internal support work that the student team did strengthened them to take on visible political advocacy in the city.

Activity:

Every leader needs to cultivate a support team. Pick five people at work whom you would like to have as members of your team. Call a meeting and talk with them about wanting to cultivate a group that learns to back each other completely. At the first meeting, team members can take turns telling what they want the others to know about them. At subsequent meetings, each member can suggest a different topic. It is important to divide the time equally so that each person has an opportunity to speak freely and to have the others listen. The commitment each person makes is to stick by the group, even when things get hard. Sometimes it is valuable to have this group made up of people with the same backgrounds. Other times it is valuable to have a diverse team. Both have advantages.

Leaders often fail through isolation and discouragement. By creating a support team of people who are committed to each other as well as to social change, leaders can sustain the long-term effort required to change institutions.

Principles in
action.

Durham, North Carolina

In the midst of a potentially contentious merger of the city and county school systems in Durham, North Carolina, Collin Rustin, the director of the NCBI Durham/Chapel Hill chapter, marshalled the resources of a local NCBI team to respond creatively to the pending merger with skills that eased community tensions and allowed various constituencies to work together on a student reassignment plan.

Prior to 1992, Durham City and County Schools operated separately, with the City Public Schools being predominately Black and under-funded and the County Public Schools being predominately White and well-funded. In 1992, the Durham County Commissioners decided to consolidate the school systems. The express reason for their action was "to provide each and every public school student, irrespective of their place of residence within Durham County, with an equal opportunity to learn and to provide in the schools an environment in which each student is encouraged and can reasonably be expected to realize his or her maximum educational potential."

The goal of the consolidation planners was to help the community answer a critical question raised by the task force on merger: How can the new school system better reflect the diversity of the community? As a whole, the student population of the new district was 54 percent Black, 44 percent White, and 2 percent other, including Asians, Native Americans, and Latinos. Yet, few of the schools in the County reflected that diversity. The pending merger would change the demographics.

Following the establishment of a new school board and school system, local officials established a task force to help develop an implementation plan with input from citizens of the entire county.

Soon, however, the board was at an impasse, since it was divided between Blacks representing city interests and Whites representing county interests. The school board turned to Collin Rustin, NCBI Director for Durham/Chapel Hill, to facilitate a dialogue among members and to assist them in drafting a reassignment plan.

As a result of Collin's work with the school board, a key school administrator became interested in the work of NCBI.

What drew the board to the work of NCBI was its upbeat, hopeful tone. Parents, teachers, and administrators from across Durham were terrified about the impending merger. They anticipated everything from total resistance to violence. They saw in NCBI a way to bring courage to a threatened community. NCBI did not target or blame teachers or parents for their concerns or fears. The NCBI staff worked diligently to model that every student, teacher, and parent, both from the city and the county schools, was important for the success of the merger. No one person or group was singled out for blame or condemnation.

The NCBI team met numerous times with the superintendent and director for professional development to help each of them think through and plan the implementation of the student reassignment process for the Fall of 1995. NCBI leaders were selected to facilitate the Task Force on Student Assignment, a process that brought together 24 diverse community leaders to develop an initial process for assigning students to schools within the newly formed system, giving appropriate consideration to neighborhoods, racial/ethnic balance, prior attendance zones, as well as other factors.

In addition to the work of the NCBI chapter director and members of the NCBI team with teachers, principals, and administrators, NCBI leaders successfully developed a team of high school student leaders who actively led workshops among the student population in the school system. The team trained 24 high school leaders to be part of the NCBI team and to lead prejudice reduction workshops for students. During 1994-95, this team of young people conducted many workshops for their peers. When the young people began to lead the work, they inspired all the teachers, parents, and administrators. If the young people could break through their fears, so could the rest of the community.

Within two years, strong, vibrant NCBI teams were in place in every school in the system, infusing the schools with a spirit to welcome diversity. The NCBI approach helped the City of Durham move through a difficult transition period without the anticipated intergroup unrest.

Healing
Ourselves

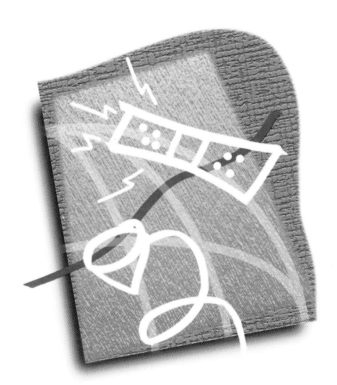

to Change
the World

Principle:

we all carry records about other groups that prevent us from building effective alliances.

Theory:

We all carry records of misinformation about people who are different than we are. The misinformation gets in the way of building close relationships.

A baby doesn't start out in the crib thinking, "I can't wait to grow up and be a racist!" Instead, little by little as each of us grows up, we learn bits and pieces of misinformation about other groups. The sources of the misinformation are all around us: television programs, movies, books, radio, magazines, billboards, conversations with friends, fleeting glimpses of strangers, and our day-to-day interactions with our families. Usually unaware, we take in all of this misinformation and it becomes part of us. The misinformation forms a type of interior recording, a literal, rigid mechanism that replays the same misinformation again and again, just as we received it. When triggered, the recorded misinformation can play in our heads, even when logic and personal experience tell us otherwise. At times, these recordings can have their own power, holding on despite our best efforts to silence them. By identifying and getting these records out into the open, we can heal from them. They then lose their power to confuse us and distort our relationships.

Example:

An African American man, the senior project engineer with an international firm, developed close, collegial relationships with the members of his staff, most of whom were White. The whole working group would routinely go out together after work for drinks, and they were often invited to each other's homes. A major overseas client commissioned the engineering staff to address a particularly difficult problem that had serious financial ramifications. The senior engineer was a world expert on the matter, and he headed the company's task force for the client. While overseas, managers from the client firm came to the White members of the team, informing them that they were reluctant to hear the presentation if it came from their Black colleague. The night before the senior engineer was scheduled to make the crucial presentation to the client's top management, his nervous White colleagues came to his hotel room. They asked him to consider not making the presentation the next morning. They suggested that since so much was riding on this contract, the client might be more receptive to the presentation if a White member of the team made the presentation instead. Both the managers of the client firm and the members of the consulting team had records that kept them from wanting to use the best person for the job.

Activity:

There is a way to identify the records that we may unwittingly carry about another group. Pick a particular racial, ethnic, or religious group. Select a partner to help you who is not a member of that group. The partner says the name of the group out loud several times. After each time say in response the very first thing that pops into your head. Do not censor or hold back. The candid, uncensored "first thoughts" indicate the type of records you've internalized. Remember in doing this activity, you may not believe or agree with your first thoughts. Nonetheless, since they've been internalized, they can still get in the way of being an ally to members of that group. We don't choose to have these records, but we can take responsibility for getting rid of them.

You may be in the process of hiring candidates for a new position. Some of the applicants may be men, women, White, or people of color. Before beginning the interviews, take a minute to examine your first thoughts toward groups that might be under represented in your workplace. This will help you to identify and then act against any records that might prevent you from being completely welcoming to all of the job candidates.

At first, it may be difficult to recognize that we have certain prejudices; but by creating a safe place to examine these "first thoughts," we can begin the process of ridding ourselves of them. We can also learn to be generous with ourselves and each other. No one actively chose to internalize misinformation about various groups. As we honestly face these internalized records, we are able to build more lasting relationships with people from many different backgrounds.

Notes

What racial, ethnic, religious or other group did you choose for the "first thoughts" exercise?

_____

_____

_____

_____

What were some of your "first thoughts?"

_____

_____

_____

_____

_____

_____

_____

_____

Principle:
effective
anti-racism leadership in the present means healing scars from the past.

Theory:

Each of us would like to believe that we have already effectively dealt with the painful experiences connected to being mistreated for who we are. But the strongest, single recurring theme in all of our leadership programs in NCBI has been that the unhealed hurts of the past make it impossible for people to lead courageously in the present. As leaders, we waffle. We don't speak up when the moment requires forthright speech. We hold back when the moment requires action. We wait for others to reach out to us first because we don't believe we're wanted. We stay locked in the safety of our own groups because we're afraid to take risks and make mistakes with other groups. All of these leadership difficulties have their roots in the past. The current situation does not need to be exactly like the past. It simply needs to have enough elements of the earlier painful experience to remind us of it. Until we've healed them, they continue to distort our vision in the present.

Example:

A newly appointed woman minister was about to have a meeting with the board of trustees of her church. There were a number of members on the board who had initially voiced concerns about the church's hiring a female pastor. Every time she thought about the upcoming meeting, she steeled herself for a battle. We asked her, "What in your own life does this situation remind you of-or when did you have similar feelings?" She said the situation reminded her of the fights she had in her own family when she was growing up. She was the only girl, and from early on, she got the message that she was not expected to succeed. Every step she had taken to develop her own leadership as a woman felt like an uphill struggle. After taking time to vent and heal some of those early messages, she realized that her battle was not with the board. So she decided to go to the meeting with an open heart. By attending the meeting relaxed and confident, not bracing for battle, she easily won the support of the few resistant board members.

Activity:

Whenever you are dealing with a leadership difficulty, the following set of questions may be helpful:

1. What is the current difficulty? Describe it with as much detail as possible.
2. When in your early life did you have a similar experience or feeling?
3. What did you need to say back then to those individuals? If you have an ally, you can use this question to let off steam about the earlier experience.

After venting, experiment with repeating the following phrase, which serves as a useful reminder that the past and present are clearly different realities.

"Once upon a time, a long, long, long time ago, I was_____(scared or angry or mistreated or unappreciated, etc.). People back then didn't understand what I needed. But that was a long, long, long time ago. And NOW, here in the present, I am _____(bold or confident or powerful or loved, etc.)." Remember that the present reality is in sharp contrast to the past, and by repeating the phrases, we can keep ourselves from becoming confused.

When we see the present as it truly is, a new moment full of limitless possibilities, then we can act creatively, free of the distortions that the past may impose.

Principle:

when we

respond to a present situation with intense emotion, we are usually acting out of a past unhealed **difficulty.**

Theory:

The fierce battles we carry on in the present often have nothing to do with the present. We can expend a great deal of energy in rehearsing the ways in which people have wronged us. We can become experts in cataloging our grievances against this person or that person. The intense focus on the present loses track of the reality that most of our present feelings can be traced to similar situations in the past. Unless we actively seek to heal the past and then clearly separate the present from the past, we are bound to repeat inappropriate behavior, responding to a past situation rather than to the present reality. The present is always new, requiring fresh solutions, unencumbered by the baggage of the past. Whenever a particular person or situation is making us excessively angry or frightened, chances are good that those reactions have only a little to do with the actual situation in the present and a whole lot to do with unhealed wrongs in the past.

Example:

Whether someone is viewing the present through an unhealed past perspective can often be found in the words used to describe a present situation, especially when the words carry passion that the present situation doesn't warrant. A supervisor was about to fire a member of her staff who had come late to work several mornings in a row. When the supervisor described the situation, she said, "I feel violated by her [the staffperson's] behavior. I can't let her mistreat me like this. After all I've done for her, she's completely abandoning me." As it turned out, this supervisor had been abandoned by a parent early in her life and tended to see the world through a lens of pending abandonment. In response to her supervisor's concerns, the staffperson said, "It's none of her business why I was late. I don't need to tell her everything about my personal life." The staffperson was raised by a domineering mother who demanded knowing her daughter's whereabouts at all times. Carrying this injury with her, the staffperson did not want to tell her supervisor that personal crises at home caused her to be late. Both the supervisor and the staffperson were playing out past unhealed patterns, which, if left unchallenged, would undermine their current work together.

Activity:

Think of a person or situation in the present that is giving you a hard time. Ask yourself the following questions:

1. Of whom (or what) does this person remind me? Your first thought in response to this question is often the most useful.
2. How is this person similar to that person (or situation)? How is this person (or situation) different? The more detailed you can answer these questions the better.
3. What do I still need to say to that person in the past that will enable me to separate that relationship from this one?
4. If I were to see the present situation as a completely new opportunity, unencumbered by past experiences, how would I take charge of it?

When we can view each present situation as a fresh, new moment, informed by the past but not bound to its repetition, we can respond creatively to what seem to be insurmountable difficulties. With this perspective, we can build both personal and professional relationships that are free of past experiences that get in the way of seeing the world as it is.

Principle:
underneath
every oppressive comment lies
some form of *injury.*

Theory:

Underneath every oppressive comment is some form of hurt. The comment is just another way of saying, "Ouch!" The more we can acquire the skill to listen without blame to an offensive comment as an expression of pain, the more readily we can become agents for change.

The link between bigotry and its origins in pain are conspicuously documented. For example, it is not coincidental that the virulent racism of the Ku Klux Klan and the efficient anti-Semitism of Nazi Germany arose in vanquished societies that suffered severe economic burdens in the aftermath of devastating wars.

When it comes to responding effectively to oppressive jokes, comments, and slurs, most people feel powerless. Yet, if we listen carefully to someone who has made an offensive remark, we offer that person space to show-often for the first time even to himself-what the underlying difficulty may be. Listening skills that lead to the transformation of one person are the same skills that lead to the transformation of thousands. If you can change one person's heart, you can change the world.

Example.

A young White man came from across the country to one of our NCBI training programs in Washington, D.C. He took public transportation to the training site, got lost, and ended up late at night in one of the District of Columbia's tough neighborhoods. The next morning, he called home and told his mother what had happened. When he mentioned how he got lost and where he ended up, his mother began to scream at him. They both got into a shouting match. She accused him of being reckless; he accused her of being racist. During the first day of the workshop, we had a chance to coach this young man. We encouraged him to see the heated exchange with his mother as a welcome opportunity for listening for the pain that lay behind his mother's reaction. That evening, when he called home, he apologized for losing his temper. He asked his mother what had been going on for her. She then told him a story he had never heard. At one time, she was a student in Washington and had dated an African American man from the neighborhood where her son had been. She said, "I loved this man, but I was always terrified going into that neighborhood-I guess, I was remembering all that terror. I was never able to look at my own racism that was fueling some of my terror. I guess you're doing that now for both of us."

Activity:

If you hear an oppressive comment, or if you notice that someone is becoming agitated, remember to listen for the pain underneath the comment. Try to step back emotionally from the encounter. With complete respect, you might ask, "I'd like to understand why you see things the way you do. Please tell me whether something in your own life experience has led you to see things this way." Then, listen. To understand that bigoted comments have their origin in some form of injury prevents us from giving up when we encounter offensive people. Instead, we can seize the opportunity for effecting change.

Principle:

people

who feed good about themselves

do not mistreat others.

Theory:

If we are serious in helping people to stop targeting other groups, we will first help them to heal the less than positive feelings they carry about themselves. Pride is different than chauvinism. Chauvinism says, "I'm better than you." But underneath, the person actually feels awful about herself. Real pride is welcoming: "I feel good about me, and I welcome you to feel just as good about you." It's hard to be an ally when you aren't feeling proud about yourself. Imagine a friend's house is on fire. You show up wanting to help but you claim, "I'm not usually very much good-I can't imagine I can do anything that will be helpful, but I'll try, even though I'm bound to fail." This is not the type of person we want around in a crisis, when quick, decisive action is required. When we feel bad about ourselves, our attention goes to our own shortcomings. Consequently, we can't be the allies that others need. Guilt and shame do not create good allies. Reclaiming pride in the things we tend to feel ashamed about is one way to become an excellent ally and a leader in welcoming diversity.

Example:

NCBI was called in to work with a school after a number of students were heard joking that they were going to burn Jews for fun over the weekend. At one point in the session, we asked the students to name groups to which they belonged of which they were proud. Several students shouted out that they were proud of being skinheads. We were amazed that immediately after boasting about being skinheads, these same students admitted, "When friends of ours tease Jews and Blacks, we don't like it, but they're our friends. We don't want to lose their friendship, so we do nothing." We were able to then teach them how to take on the anti-Semitism and racism among their friends. After giving these students a chance to claim pride in the one identity through which they were able to assert their self-worth, they were able to open up to us more honestly about their attitudes toward racism and anti-Semitism.

Activity:

The work on feeling good about ourselves is crucial preventive work in combatting all forms of oppression. If we listen carefully to ourselves and to the people in our lives, we will recognize where all of us still struggle with shame. When you hear a colleague or a co-worker struggling in this area, you can provide a useful contradiction. For example, if an older supervisor discounts her authority by saying, "But what does an old person like me know?" You might say, "You know plenty, and all of us our lucky to be able to rely on your wealth of experiences."

You might consider coming to a mutual understanding with one other person at work. With this "buddy" you can both agree to interrupt any demeaning comments that either of you direct at yourselves.

People who feel good about themselves can confidently direct their energies to constructive efforts.

Principle:

when

witnessing oppressive behavior, having a chance to vent leads to clearer thinking about what is useful to do next.

Theory:

When we hear oppressive jokes, comments, or slurs, or when someone has said something to us that upsets us, we are often not able to think of an effective, immediate response. Sometimes we can be so angry that all we want to do is just strike the other person. Other times we're simply so stunned that we don't know what to do or say—we freeze in silence. Clearly, it rarely makes sense to attack another person. So it is helpful to have an ally who understands the need for venting and to have a place to go, away from the person who made the oppressive comment, to say the unpleasant things we would like to say. Creating the space to vent our outrage allows us to reclaim our thinking, to return to the offensive person in the future with a clearer head, ready to implement an effective communication strategy that is more likely to achieve the results we want.

Example:

A few years ago Cherie Brown and I were working together in Ireland. NCBI had been invited to lead Protestant and Roman Catholic reconciliation work in the North. Cherie is Jewish and I am Roman Catholic. A Protestant minister from Dublin invited us to spend the first night in Ireland at his home. The minister, though eager to be supportive of the reconciliation effort, had not met either of us before, and he did not know our religious backgrounds. After we settled into our rooms, the minister invited us into the parlor for cake and tea. While he poured strong Irish tea we talked about religion in Ireland. At one point the minister said, "I don't think I ever met any Jews—they're such a weird people. I don't even know why they exist anymore." Cherie froze. She was so taken aback by the comment that she was unable to say anything. I tried to get him to talk about his experiences with Jews, but the minister said he had none. Later that evening, Cherie asked me privately, if she could have a few minutes to vent about what the minister had said. I encouraged Cherie to direct her fury at me, while I took on the role of the minister. Muffling the sound with a pillow so our host would not hear, Cherie screamed, "How could you say such a thing to me? Don't you know that I'm a Jew? It's not me but people like you who don't deserve to exist." After venting for a while, Cherie decided that she would try something new the next day. At breakfast the following morning, Cherie asked the minister about his religion, what drew him to the ministry, and why it was so important to him. Then, in a completely relaxed way, she talked about her pride in being Jewish and what it was like to find so few Jews in Ireland. The minister genuinely expressed interest and listened carefully to what she had to say.

—G.J.M.

Activity:

After someone has made an oppressive joke, comment, or slur, find a friend or ally who will spend a few minutes with you. Ask her to repeat the offensive comment. While she is repeating the offensive comment, she can offer you her hands. Putting your hands on top of hers, shake them, saying the least polite thing you would like to say to the person who made the offensive comment. Of course, these are not the things you would ever actually say to that person, but it is helpful to get them out.

Venting with an ally in a safe, controlled environment can open emotional space, leading to fresh, creative thinking.

Principle:
diversity
leadership requires
reclaiming *courage.*

Theory:

When we were little, many of us spoke up about the injustices we noticed. Yet, early on, we were silenced. We were told we should be quiet or we did not understand or we should just go to our rooms. Sometimes we were told we were being rude when we were just pointing out the truth. We quickly learned to hide our opinions, to turn the other way when injustices took place. Our commitment to speak the truth may lie buried beneath layer upon layer of powerlessness and silence. The ways we have been taught to be polite can also at times be the glue that holds prejudice in place. Many of us need to reclaim our strong, early voices, remembering our indignation and our ability to speak up.

Example:

A five-year-old White friend of ours attended a diverse, multi-racial kindergarten. He happened to be at a party with his family where only White people were present. This wasn't his usual world. In his characteristic, honest way, he looked around the room and said to his mother in a loud, booming voice, "Mommy, why aren't there any Black people here?" His mother was horrified that he was so direct, and she quickly told him to be quiet. Whenever this boy noticed racism as a young child and said something about it, he was silenced. He was told he was being rude or disrespectful. By the time he was 10, the feelings of powerlessness had taken their toll. An African American boy was being teased on the playground and our friend remained silent. He told us afterwards how devastated he felt because he didn't do anything in the face of open racism.

Activity:

Remember a time when you were young and spoke up against any kind of injustice. Perhaps it was something that was going on at home. Were you welcomed for having a loud, courageous voice? Were you encouraged to speak up for yourself? Next, think of a time when you had difficulty speaking up against injustice, when you had trouble being courageous. Ask yourself, if you knew you were completely powerful, if you knew you could make a profound difference, what would you have done differently? Our ability to speak up in the present will be based on undoing the messages from the past that taught us to remain silent in face of the wrongs we witnessed.

When we are able to see what gets in the way of acting courageously, we can take the incremental steps to become more powerful. We need only recognize that we already have the power to take control, not only of our lives but also of the world around us.

Principle:

being

an ally to another group requires us to heal the negative messages we have internalized about our own group.

Theory:

When most people think about building an environment that welcomes diversity, they tend to think about doing work across group lines. This is, of course, a key part of doing diversity work. But it is equally important to work on "internalized oppression," the less than positive messages we have received about the members of our own group. It is hard to build unity across group lines when there are intense divisions within our own group. There are many examples of internalized oppression: a woman who says she'd never work for a woman boss, an African American who thinks that if you want good medical attention you should see a White doctor, a Jew who thinks that most other Jews are pushy. We internalize the stereotyped messages about members of our own group, and then we either adopt those stereotypic attitudes toward members of our own group, or we blame our group for their difficulties. We are often ashamed of those members who in any way act out the stereotypes. Internalized oppression can be one of the most painful blocks to effective coalition-building work.

Example:

Several NCBI staff were working with a group of high school students in Birmingham, Alabama, training them in how to take leadership in their schools, especially on how to reduce intergroup polarization and student unrest. School administrators had initiated the training program in the wake of a number of racial incidents in the schools. At one point in the training program, Alvin Herring, Chief Operating Director of NCBI, asked the young people, "Who are the real leaders in your school?" Instead of putting up their own hands in response to his question, every young person pointed to all of the adults in the room. The young people were caught by internalized oppression.

Parents, teachers, other adults, and even other young people let young people know every day that they are not powerful, that they're incapable of leading the world. Young people internalize these messages. As a result, when it comes to ending racism and other forms of oppression, they don't look to each other for leadership. When well-intended adults tell young people that they are the leaders of tomorrow, the adults, as well as some young people, overlook the fact that young people are already leaders of the world today.

Activity:

Think about a group to which you belong that you'd like to identify and then heal your less than positive feelings about some members of that group. Then, imagine a friend (it doesn't matter whether he or she is a member of your group or not) who has supported you in the past. As you picture that person listening to you, say all the things you can't stand about some members of your own group. Some of us have been told never to criticize our own people, so saying our negative feelings can be a stretch. After you've had a chance to release the negative internalized recordings, think of the many things you love about that same group. List the many things of that group of which you are proud. For some, being delighted with one's own group is easy; for others, the internalized recordings may be so strong that the effort to reclaim pride in one's own group can pose a serious challenge. To find what we are proud of in our own group after voicing our negative comments may help to heal the internalized recordings of shame.

Many people have found that setting up a support group of similarly situated people can be a great help, especially when the groups are work-related. Some employers may actually sponsor such groups as a way to keep newcomers involved in the organization. Instead of being divisive, fostering voluntary support groups can demonstrate the company's commitment to welcoming members of certain groups and creating a workplace environment that is responsive to their needs. Though many may think that separate organizations in the workplace based on sex or race or ethnicity undermine the cohesiveness of an organization, usually the opposite occurs. The voluntary support groups provide a way for many people who would otherwise feel alienated to belong to the larger organization and contribute to its broader mission.

When you are more united with your own group, you can be more effective in building coalitions across group lines.

Notes

Pick a racial, ethnic, religious or other group to which you belong. Which group did you pick?

_____

_____

_____

_____

What are some of the things you can't stand about your group?

_____

_____

_____

_____

What are some of the things you love about the same group?

_____

_____

_____

_____

Principle:

healing
discouragement leads to

more effective *activism.*

Theory:

There are many urgent social and political issues that require immediate attention. Racism and other forms of oppression, including economic injustices, will not go away without a lot of hard work. Social activism, however, often increases when activists have an opportunity to voice the feelings of discouragement that often accompany doing social-change work. When confronted with failed efforts, many dedicated activists in the '60s never had the chance to work through their discouragement. As a result, many burnt out, giving up activist commitments and settling for small lives with individualistic goals. Without grieving losses and gaining a renewed sense of hope, it can be almost impossible to sustain a life-long commitment to social activism. People will not eagerly follow our leadership if we are continually under stress, lonely, and burdened by our focus on what still needs to be done. To the extent we can care for ourselves, especially in restoring ourselves, we can model how to care for others.

Example:

A group of Jewish activists, many of whom had spent more than a decade on building support for Arab-Jewish cooperation within the United States, gathered for a weekend conference I was leading. Many of them were extremely discouraged, because peace efforts in the Middle East had broken down. I canceled the planned session for Saturday evening and replaced it with an open dialogue. One person after the next expressed weariness. They all said that they were hopeless about seeing peace in the Middle East in their lifetimes. One person finally voiced the discouragement so many were feeling: She wept as she said, "All of our hard work has been in vain." I went home the next day thinking I had failed. I was convinced that the Saturday night session with all its hopelessness would set back Middle East peace efforts even further. I was surprised then when I received phone calls and mail from conference participants, all of them saying how useful the conference had been. One man wrote, "I was feeling totally hopeless and now I'm ready to go forward. I've been able to take on far more work since that Saturday night session." The feelings of hopelessness in themselves were not holding people back. Rather, it was the isolation-having no one with whom to share the grief connected to dashed dreams-that had slowed down their efforts.

—C.R.B.

Activity:

Think about a social or political matter that you are currently working on, one that may cause you some measure of hopelessness. Ask yourself the following questions:

1. Have I been taking the time to deal with the feelings of discouragement, or have I just been moving forward, hoping the discouragement will simply disappear?
2. Do I set aside time to talk to someone who can listen to my discouragement?
3. Do I work in complete isolation or can I confide in someone?

Many managers, supervisors, and others in leadership roles mistakenly assume that isolation goes with the job. Having a place to voice feelings of hopelessness can break the isolation and allow for more effective leadership.

Principles in

action

Allentown, Pennsylvania

Relying on the support of allies, Nilima Patel, a member of the NCBI team in Allentown, Pennsylvania, was able to take leadership in her community in fighting against the oppression of Asian women.

Nilima, who is of Indian heritage, was raised in Nairobi, Kenya, until she was 16 years old. At first, her family resisted the idea of spending money on the education of women. However, they eventually decided to send her to England and later to Canada to complete her education. In 1975, she got married and moved to India, but she was discouraged by the sexism she encountered. She was young, outspoken, and Western educated, but no one took her seriously, especially men. In 1991, she moved to Allentown.

When the Leadership for Diversity Initiative (LDI) steering committee recruited Nilima to be part of the Allentown team, she was working at a local bank. She was the first person of color in her position, but she felt invisible, a token of the bank's affirmative action efforts. She was especially surprised to find that White women, whom she expected to be her allies, failed to back her.

To be released from work to participate in the three-year NCBI leadership program, Nilima needed the backing of her employer. At first she was hesitant, but by working on her concerns in healing sessions with the NCBI team of community leaders, she was able to win the support of the bank.

Nilima was a member of an Indian association, a social and cultural organization, founded in 1972, serving several hundred families in the Lehigh Valley. She would speak out about how Indian women were often mistreated. From men she heard that she shouldn't shame the community, speaking so negatively about how Indian men treat Indian women. From Indian women, even from the most powerful, she heard that she didn't know what she was talking about. The criticism she encountered made her want to give up, it reminded her of the paternalism she had encountered during her time in India. However, with the support of the NCBI team, she was able to remember that the present and the past were independent realities; and with healing she could reclaim her own power as an Indian woman. As a result, she decided that she did not have to remain a victim within the organization. She decided to take visible leadership in the organization, which previously had only male officials. At every opportunity, she advanced her views about the equality of women and the ways in which Indians encountered racism. With the encouragement from her NCBI team leaders, she ran for the vice presidency of the organization and won. Yet, when she became vice president, she became discouraged when she overheard the ex-president say to the president, "How did she get this? A woman can't hold this position." However, she was determined not to let such negative comments deter her.

With the support of the NCBI team, she continued to take active, public leadership in the community. At a 1996 Hindu youth conference, which was held at a local Hindu temple, which Nilima attended, many of the Indian girls told her, "You are so cool. We would support the work you [NCBI] are doing."

A crucial turning point for Nilima came when she met NCBI's Asian constituency leader Raj Chawla, a man of Indian heritage, at the NCBI Associates meeting in 1996. Having heard Nilima's hurts around sexism, he said he was willing to do his own work as an Indian man to clean up the sexism he had. He also made a commitment to her that he would do whatever it took to end sexism. Raj was a contradiction for her: She had never before found an Asian man who was willing to recognize and work on sexism and completely back her leadership as a powerful woman.

In 1997, Nilima was invited to speak at a Martin Luther King, Jr. Day celebration. She spoke about her experiences of discrimination as an Indian woman. Afterward, several employees where she worked told her that they had been unaware of the discrimination that Indian women faced and promised to support her in the future. She also asked for and got support from a senior human resources officer.

Most recently, Nilima was involved in working with Indian young people. She organized a day-long prejudice reduction workshop for young people between the ages of 14 and 21. She worked hard to recruit Indian young people to attend the workshop. As part of the recruitment effort, she called several parents and explained to them the need for young people to work on the forms of oppression that target them. Many of the parents told her openly that they didn't see a need for such a program. They claimed none of their young people experienced racism. Again, she was about to give up. Instead, she pulled together a small group of allies from the NCBI team, vented her frustration about an apparently hopeless situation, and moved on. Armed with renewed confidence, she was able to win over the reluctant parents, and the workshop took place.

During the workshop, the young people worked on two key issues: adultism and racism. Adultism is the mistreatment or dismissal of young people based on their age. In a particularly significant moment in the day, the young people prepared a report of all the things they never wanted adults to say, think, or do to them again. They spoke about the pressures that led two Indian youths to commit suicide. In regard to racism, they felt that parents, while seeing their children working hard and doing well in school, trivialized or overlooked the fact that their children had to deal with racist incidents again and again.

Building on success after success, with the healing support of the Allentown NCBI team, Nilima is reclaiming her power as an Indian woman and taking leadership in the Lehigh Valley.

Becoming

Effective
Allies

Principle:

human
beings want to be allies to each *other.*

Theory:

We inherently want to be allies to people from many different groups. The places where we have difficulty being effective allies for each other are the same places where we have been hurt ourselves. There are two important ways to increase our effectiveness as allies. First, despite the pull to self-criticism, it is important to take stock of the times when we succeeded in being an effective ally. We rarely increase our effectiveness by dwelling on all of the things we still need to get right. This principle is especially important for those of us who are seeking allies. Pointing out only how the people around us have failed usually only increases their discouragement. Remembering the successes can lead to increased confidence and a greater ability to be an effective ally. Second, to increase our effectiveness as an ally, we must identify and then heal the places where we have also been mistreated. We cannot expect to be successful in standing up for someone else if we have not already learned how to stand up for ourselves.

Example:

A college student at one of our training sessions was actively involved in anti-racism work on his campus. He particularly wanted to increase his effectiveness at being an ally to Latinos. When we asked him to think about a time when he'd experienced mistreatment, he spoke about his experiences growing up as an overweight boy. He'd been beaten up every day for years by a number of older boys and called hateful names. He had very few friends. We then asked him to describe a time when he'd effectively stood up against the oppression of Latinos. He proudly told us about how he'd organized all his friends to attend a major rally against discrimination on his campus. Next, we asked him to describe a situation where he'd not been able to stand up against discrimination. He remembered a time with his friends that included racial jokes and bantering. He wanted desperately to say something, but he was afraid that he'd lose his friends. He hated himself for being silent, but fear kept him frozen. Only after he was able to identify and then heal from the early experiences when he was beaten up, was he able to reclaim his power and take on the racist jokes of his friends. Afterward, he reported back to us that the next time his friends told racist jokes, he was able to interrupt them. He was able to push through the fear that had silenced him.

Activity:

Pick a group for whom you would like to be a more effective ally and answer the following questions:
1. When was a time that you experienced painful discrimination or mistreatment?
2. When was a time that you were an ally to the group you have chosen? Remember that there are many ways of being an ally. For example, you might focus on a time when you learned more information about that group or on a time when you built a closer relationship to a member of that group.
3. When was a time that you were not the ally you hoped to be?
4. What is similar in your answers to questions 1 and 3?

When we understand that the source of our difficulty in being an effective ally lies in our experience of mistreatment, we can stop blaming ourselves and channel our energies into doing what we can to stand up on behalf of others.

Principle:

one-on-one

relationship-building is at the heart of

effective intergroup coalitions.

Theory:

The primary work of coalition-building is establishing personal relationships. We don't build a relationship with a program or an idea. We build a relationship with a person who is committed to a particular program or idea. Relationship-building has been seen traditionally as "women's work," and not surprisingly, given the nature of sexism, it has been undervalued. Yet, one-on-one relationship-building is the catalyst for institutional change. We don't change institutions, we change individuals who set policies for institutions.

Example:

I was leading a program in Birmingham, Alabama, in the 16th Street Baptist Church, the place where in 1963 several Black children were killed by a racially motivated bombing. At one point in the day, a White woman who taught at the University of Birmingham put up her hand and asked pointedly, "Can you help me, I feel like the Black students in my classroom let me into the living room, but not into the kitchen?" I have often thought about that comment. Living rooms are polite. Living rooms are formal, where we are on our best behavior, stiffly entertaining the people from down the block. Living rooms are where we learn to be tolerant. Kitchens are where we are family. Kitchens are where we "get down" with each other. Kitchens are where we come uninvited, because we know we belong. Kitchens are also the place where we can fight and still come back, never doubting that we are welcome. Diversity work is ultimately about increasing the diversity of people who live with us in our kitchens.

—*C.R.B.*

Activity:

Do not undervalue the simple, social ways of building relationships. An intergroup coalition can begin with the decision to get close to one other person. Consider the people in your neighborhood whom you'd like to know better. Take the initiative. Who is there in your office or organization with whom you would like to make a better connection? Focus on one person, perhaps that person comes from a different race or ethnic background, and suggest having lunch together. Making a friend as a strategy to deal with discrimination may sound like a well-intended, polite way to side-step complex social issues. But the work it takes to make and then keep a close relationship with one other person can be arduous. It may involve overcoming initial awkwardness, stepping outside of one's own comfortable isolation, facing the fear of rejection, moving beyond politeness to genuine conversation, revealing struggles, dealing with misunderstandings, and sticking by each other when it may be difficult. The place where all of us acquire the skills to lead are in our relationships with other people.

Principle:
risk-taking
and mistake-making are essential

for building close relationships

across group *lines.*

Theory:

Most of us learned early in life, particularly in school, that we had to get things right the first time. Good grades are based on answering the questions correctly. Yet, there's no way we're going to break through all the barriers that get in the way of close relationships across race, ethnicity, gender, social class, religion, disability, age, and sexual orientation without asking questions, often saying things that may not make sense. We must put into practice a dual commitment. First, we have to give ourselves permission to take risks and make mistakes around others; second, we have to be generous toward others when they make mistakes about us or our people. An NCBI definition of an ally is someone who makes a mistake and sticks around to clean it up.

Example:

A father and his school-aged sons went shopping one Saturday at the local grocery store. While the father was busy gathering the items from his grocery list, his sons caught sight of another shopper in the same aisle, a man with a forearm prosthesis that ended with a metal hook. Recalling the character Captain Hook in a recent movie version of the Peter Pan story, the boys shouted out, "Hey, Dad, look it's Hook!" Their father glanced down the aisle, noticed the man, and became mortified, knowing that the man had heard his sons' comment. Instead of glaring at them and walking away, the man came toward the boys. He asked them if they wanted to see his hook. In a relaxed way, he was able to give the boys information about how his prosthesis worked and why he used it.

Activity:

From childhood we are trained not to point fingers and not to ask nosy questions, less someone take offense. You can now give yourself permission to ask people questions about themselves. Most people are eager to talk about themselves, if only someone would ask. If you are trying to get closer to another person, don't shy away from asking questions. Here are a sample of the kind of questions that you may have always wanted to ask. To someone of African Heritage, you might inquire whether that person has a preference for the term Black or African American. To someone of Jewish heritage, you might ask what it's like for that person during the Christmas season when virtually every public place is decorated for Christmas. To someone in a wheelchair, you might ask what that person prefers-should you offer assistance or should you assume that the person is self-sufficient. We don't know everything about each other. We only get closer by making the effort, by overcoming our own awkwardness, venturing to ask questions, and making mistakes.

The most effective leaders are risk-takers, people who are not afraid to try something new and to learn from correcting mistakes.

Principle:
we can
choose our attitude toward

what we *hear.*

Theory:

We may not have control over what people say and when they say it. But we do have control over our attitudes. We can choose our perspective. Instead of thinking, "Oh, no! I have to listen once again to all of this painfully abusive talk," we can decide, "This is a wonderful opportunity to make contact with someone, to have a useful and open dialogue about a challenging issue-this might be an opportunity to shift someone's attitude." The first way of thinking leaves us powerless, whereas the second gives us power. By holding onto the reality that we can continue to think, we can create opportunities for a dialogue leading to change.

Example:

A Korean American mediator was asked to work with a Washington neighborhood in which a conflict arose between African American residents and Korean American merchants. The Black community decided to boycott Korean shops in the aftermath of the killing of a Black teenager. The young man was in the process of robbing a small Korean shop when the owner shot him. The mediator met with an African American woman, who was a leader in the neighborhood. The woman screamed, "You come into our neighborhoods, and you have no concern for our community. You just take our money and run." Instead of attacking back or challenging the woman, the mediator responded, "This is exactly the kind of honest dialogue I've been looking to hear. I'm so glad you're telling me all this. I want to know more." Later, the Korean American mediator commented, "I don't think this was what she expected to hear from someone with an Asian face like mine, because the woman looked at me in complete shock. But then, the African American woman shifted, she said, `You know, I do know how your people must feel. Some of these young kids come into the neighborhood and have no respect for anyone, even for their own people. We both, Koreans and Blacks in the neighborhood, need to figure out what to do together.'"

Activity:

Welcome whatever negative comments come your way. See every barb as a gem: Someone has chosen to hand you an opportunity. Cultivate the attitude that you are lucky when someone hands you an offensive comment, because you can't wait to experiment in handling it in a way that can lead to genuine change. Remember some of the comments you have heard and how you might respond in a tone of genuine interest. For example, if your neighbor often says, "Those people are taking over our neighborhood." The next time she makes the comment, you can be ready. You might respond, "I'm so glad you brought that up. I've been wondering-why do we have so many feelings about people from overseas who have come to our country?" Stepping beyond powerlessness, it is possible to choose an attitude that makes you in charge of any situation.

Principle: **we don't** change people's minds. We change their hearts with personal stories of *discrimination.*

Theory:

Many of us have tried at great length to change someone's bigoted attitude. We try to convince them by pointing out the errors in their position. We try to give them new information. In the end, we walk away frustrated, assured that some people will just never change. New information rarely changes people, but hearing personal stories of discrimination can transform the most hardened hearts. We can refute facts and figures, but we can't refute someone's story. Authentic stories of the heart have their own reasons that can be more persuasive than the most carefully crafted arguments. We don't change people's minds; we change their hearts.

Example:

In a straw poll at a community meeting prior to the city council's vote on a Gay rights ordinance, the principal of one of the largest high schools in the U.S. Southwest spoke out against the measure. Shortly afterward, a Lesbian parent came forward and told the agonizing story of her recent court battle to maintain custody of her daughter. Despite all of the evidence that she marshalled to demonstrate that she provided her daughter with a stable and loving home, her ex-husband claimed that she was an unfit mother because she was a Lesbian. The ex-husband prevailed in court, and as a result, he won sole custody of their daughter. Immediately following the court ruling, he moved out of state with their daughter, leaving no forwarding address or any other means to contact them. When this woman finished her story, the high school principal stood up. He said that while he was listening, he found himself thinking about all of the parents of children in his school who showed no interest in their children-some even beat them. Yet, here was a mother who grieved over the loss of her involvement in her daughter's life. Who was he, he asked, to deny this woman her right to be a parent? Touched by the story, he shifted his position and he publicly committed himself to work toward passage of the pending civil rights ordinance.

Activity:

When you observe people fiercely arguing their positions on an issue, you may help them by trying to get them to speak about the issue in a personal way. In a light, interested tone you might ask one of the following questions:
1.   "You sure have a lot of passion about this topic. What in particular in your life has led to your deep concern about this issue?"
2.   "Please help me understand what this issue means to you. Has something happened in your life that has led you to come to this conclusion?"

The goal of these questions is to help people shift from articulating positions to sharing the personal experiences that led to the formation of the positions.

A personal story is a powerful tool to effect change. Personal stories of discrimination can link people who differ and create shifts in attitudes where other approaches failed. Even if hearing a personal story does not change someone's attitude, it may help us recognize the humanity in another person's position. We are then more likely to stay in the room and work out where we differ.

Principle:

listening
is not the same as *agreeing.*

Theory:

Too often, we make the mistake of equating listening with agreeing. In public, many of us intuitively react to vocal opposition by taking a firm stance, sensing that any dissent in an open forum will undermine our agenda. In private, we may be afraid that if we do not immediately register our disapproval of another person's point of view, then our silence may convey a tacit endorsement of what we may consider an objectionable opinion. Neither is true. Listening is not a sign of weakness, a stance adopted only by the powerless. Instead, listening can be a revolutionary act, leading to unforeseen possibilities.

Example:

As a Jewish woman, I was invited many years ago to speak at a conference with an Arab colleague on Arab-Jewish cooperation. The ballroom where we were speaking was packed. In the course of my presentation, I said that I was proud of Israel. A Lebanese woman, who was seated in the back of the ballroom, stood up and cut me off in mid-sentence. She shouted, "How dare you be proud of Israel!" The Lebanese woman had worked in the PLO camps in southern Lebanon. She was in the United Sates for surgery on her ears, since her hearing had become impaired as a result of Israel's bombing of southern Lebanon. For the next 15 minutes the woman listed in an angry, confrontational tone all of the atrocities she believed Israel had done to the Palestinian people. With some of the things she said I agreed; with other things she said I did not. Most painful were her accusations that echoed past charges that had been used to attack Jews. I did not stop her. I did not interrupt her or ask her to sit down in the interest of time. I did not refute her points one by one. I listened. I knew it was important to model being a Jewish woman who wanted to listen to an Arab woman. At the end of her 15 minute monologue, the woman stopped and looked at me as though she were seeing me for the first time. She lowered her voice and from across the room, she said, "You're the first Jewish person who has ever listened to me. Can we meet for lunch?" The lunch led to our work together leading some of the first sessions ever held between members of the PLO and Israeli Jews.

—C.R.B.

Activity:

When you find yourself in a situation where someone is saying something with which you strongly disagree, resist the urge to have your say. You have a choice. You can either keep your attention focused on the other person, or you can give in to the pull to want to set the other person right. Choose to put your attention on the other person. Relax, do not interrupt or comment. Give the other person as much time and attention as she needs to finish saying whatever she wants to say. Instead of volunteering your opinion, keep the other person talking. Try to listen so long and so well that the person with whom you disagree asks you what you think.

Power does not reside in silencing opposition but in creating within ourselves the ability to listen to people with whom we disagree. The ability to listen is an act of leadership that can effect change.

Principle:

to move

a conflict forward, there is no room

for two hurts at the same time.

Theory:

Bridge-building work across group lines requires conflict resolution skills. Conflicts often erupt when two people who are hurting clash with each other. To move the conflict toward resolution, one person can take charge of the situation by deciding to put his own issues aside for the moment and to listen to the concerns of the other party.

Example:

A couple were guests at a hotel and noticed that there was a large statue of the Indian mascot of the local university in the lobby of the hotel. They were offended by the statue, because they felt it was insulting to Native American peoples. The couple went immediately to the manager of the hotel and demanded that he remove it. The manager became defensive and refused to remove the statue. A month later, another guest at the hotel who was attending an NCBI session also found the statue offensive. He went to the same manager and made the same request. But he approached the manager in a different way. He began by acknowledging how much he appreciated the hotel management and staff. He expressed his concerns about the statue without criticizing the manager. He assumed the best of the manager, expecting the manager to do the right thing. The manager responded by saying, "You know, someone just last month came to me with the same complaint, but they were hostile and I decided to ignore their request. But after listening to you, I've learned something, and I'm going to remove the statue." When we come at people with our own painful emotions it's often very hard for them to hear the legitimacy of our concerns. When we listen to them, it is much easier for them to hear our concerns in return.

Activity:

When you know you are going to have a discussion with someone at work about a topic that you suspect will readily upset you both, decide to put aside your initial upset and try to listen. It will then be much easier for the other person to listen to you. The following phrases may help:

> *"It looks like we're both upset-why don't you tell me what's going on for you."*

> *"I'd like to know more about how you see this matter."*

> *"I can tell this is important to you, and I sincerely want to understand how you see things."*

If you can momentarily put your own concerns aside to listen to another person's point of view, you are more likely to find a mutually agreeable way to accomplish your own ultimate goal.

Principle:
you can
develop sound policies on controversial issues when you understand the heartfelt concerns on all sides.

Theory:

Principled people can legitimately disagree with each other. However, when we find ourselves in the midst of a heated controversy, we can quickly forget that the other side might have a legitimate concern, informed by life experiences, that we are unable to hear. We can become so invested in defending our own positions that we fail to listen to what the other party is actually saying. Consequently, we often miss the common ground we share and the opportunity to cooperate on a common agenda.

Example:

Two close friends, Anne and Peter, could not even bring up the subject of abortion without slipping into an argument. Amid the highly charged public rhetoric on the topic, each had come to a decision on the matter-and each had a hard time hearing what the other was saying. They both decided to slow down the recurring argument they had on this issue. Taking turns, each tried to state what led them to their conclusions. Anne was concerned with the lives of young, single, poor women. She argued that once these women became pregnant, the burden of child-rearing made their lives enormously difficult. She believed that women would continue to have abortions even if they were illegal. They would simply become more dangerous. She explained that as a woman she constantly battled sexism, having to overcome the assumption that what women think and what women want is unimportant. Peter was concerned about the value society placed on human life. He compared the practice of widespread abortion on demand to the historic decision to use nuclear weapons. According to Peter, who was a pacifist, the deployment of nuclear weapons in World War II had profound consequences, reaching far beyond even the horrific immediate devastation of the blast. He argued that as a result of this political decision, the value of human life had been significantly diminished everywhere. Peter was concerned that current abortion policies had similar far-reaching consequences, eroding the value of human life in both known and unknown ways. In listening to each other, Anne and Peter did not change their positions, but they heard for the first time that each of them came to this issue with a genuine concern for enhancing the quality of human lives. They also found that they no longer wanted to demonize each other's positions.

Activity:

In dealing with a controversial issue involving two parties, you may find the following six-step process helpful in moving the disagreement forward:

1. Without interrupting or planning a rebuttal while the other person is speaking, listen carefully to what the person is saying.
2. Repeat back to the person who has just spoken—in the exact words, if possible—the precise reasons the other person gave for her opinion.
3. Next, ask her a question that communicates that you value her opinion and want to know more about how she sees the issue. For example, you might ask, "Please tell me more how you see this matter-is there anything from your own background that has led you to this conclusion?"
4. The parties then switch roles and repeat the first three steps.

5. Write down the concerns of both persons, checking with them to make sure that the recorded concerns accurately reflect their respective positions.

6. Review both persons' concerns, pointing out the areas of agreement. Then, propose a reframed question that takes at least one concern from each side into account. A reframed question often follows the format, "How can we do X, while at the same time doing Y?" For example, in the abortion dispute between Anne and Peter mentioned above, you might ask, "How can we guarantee that young disadvantaged women are not burdened by pregnancy and child-care, while taking measures that will keep abortion from becoming a population control policy that ultimately devalues human life?" The refrained question moves the controversy forward, inviting fresh thinking on the issue by incorporating each side's concern.

Controversies do not have to degenerate into polarization. A well-formulated reframed question can ensure the development of polices that take into account the best thinking of all sides.

Notes

Choose a controversial issue and trace the development of how two differing points of view relate to each other through the 6 steps listed above.

_____

_____

_____

_____

_____

_____

_____

_____

_____

_____

Principle:
reach
for the higher ground.

Theory:

We begin with the assumption that human beings are always doing the best they can under any given circumstances. No one wakes up in the morning wanting to be ineffective. Therefore, there is no room for blame, but plenty of room for reminding people how good they are and how well they are already doing. Often, all that is needed to transform a difficult situation is to hold out the reasonable expectation that people will act in tune with their best selves.

Example:

Alvin Herring, the Chief Operating Director of NCBI, and I were returning home to Washington after leading an NCBI program in the Mid-West. We had a change in flights at Chicago. While we were waiting for our flight, we saw a mother traveling with two young children, a boy and girl. They were waiting at the gate next to ours. The mother lost her temper and smacked the girl hard across the face. The daughter shrieked, tears flowed down her cheeks. The other passengers in the area muffled gasps, fidgeted in their seats, and cast their eyes toward the floor. Al and I turned to each other and decided that we had to do something. We went up to the mother and I said, "Having a hard day?" The mother answered, "I'm having a horrible day. My husband couldn't be with us. The kids are fighting and they're driving me crazy." While Al continued to listen to the mother, I struck up a conversation with the little girl. "Having a tough time?" I said. With the added attention, the girl sobbed hard. Quivering, she said, "My mother blames me for everything! It was my brother's fault!" Both mother and daughter had our attention. We listened to them without offering advice. We learned what was going on for each of them, and in the process both relaxed. It only took five minutes. Shortly, the airline announced the boarding of their flight. The mother and son said good-by and waived as they started off down the jetway. While giving a thumbs-up sign, I whispered to the little girl, "Now take good care of your little brother." Beaming, she returned my sign, and with her head high she skipped after her mother onto the plane.

—C.R.B.

Activity:

When you assume the best of others, they will often rise to meet your expectations. Just as with the mother in the airport, it is often impossible to see all of the things with which another person is contending. In a tense situation, one way of breaking an impasse is to remember how good the other person is and how hard he may be struggling to do the right thing. For example, you might say, "I know how committed you are to having this project go well, and I appreciate how much effort you are putting into working things out with me."

It never weakens us to be generous, to assume the best of each other. Prejudice reduction work requires tremendous patience and generosity. We never know all the difficulties that another person is bearing.

Principle:

building

*allies with people who belong to groups
that have traditionally mistreated our
people is a powerful way to break
the cycle of* mistrust.

Theory:

When we belong to a group that has experienced a long history of mistreatment (e.g., women, Jews, people of color, working people, people with disabilities, Gays and Lesbians, etc.), it is often hard for us to build close, trusting relationships with people who belong to the groups that have traditionally mistreated our people. When we are around these groups, we may remain wary, waiting to see whether a member of the group will say or do something to confirm our worst suspicions. Anytime a member of that group doesn't indicate a perfect willingness to be an ally we hold onto the memory long after the incident is over. Despite our best efforts, we cannot conceal the mistrust. In turn, our potential allies notice our distance and conclude that since we're holding back, we obviously don't want them. Consequently, they stop trying to be our allies. Their lack of effort then only reconfirms our belief that they were untrustworthy in the first place.

There is no more powerful way to break through this cycle of mistrust than to build a close relationship with someone who belongs to a group that has historically mistreated our people. The challenge is to stay close, past the point where we feel we can no longer trust.

Example:

A firefighters union was about to split apart when Black firefighters began to organize a separate union. White and Black firefighters were openly hostile to each other. The dispute was undermining morale, affecting the ability of the firefighters to work together as a team-a result with potentially disastrous consequences, since the firefighters needed to rely on each other in responding to life-threatening emergencies in the community. The union called a meeting to try to bridge the differences. One of the African American firefighters, who played a key role in establishing the Black firefighters union, fought back tears as he told his White colleagues that his father had always wanted to be a firefighter but Jim Crow laws prevented him. With his father's history in mind, he said that he still found it hard to trust that his White colleagues would care about the needs of Black firefighters. Then, a White firefighter spoke. He was Irish and an ex-Marine. All his relatives as far back as he knew had been firefighters. It's all he'd ever wanted to be. He was convinced that a separate Black firefighters union would divide the union and keep him from doing the only job he'd ever wanted to do. After they listened to each other, they decided to come up with a strategy to increase trust between White and Black firefighters. The Black firefighters union invited the White firefighter to their meeting. He sat at the head table as an honored guest. The head of the Black firefighters union came to the next meeting of the whole union and explained the specific needs of the Black firefighters. The two men decided that they would model for both groups what it means to trust each other.

Activity:

Choose one person at work or in your community who belongs to a group you tend to mistrust because that group has historically mistreated your people. Set a goal each week of reaching out in new ways to befriend that person. You might try saying to yourself the following phrase before each encounter: "I will treat this person as if he or she were eager to be my dependable friend and ally." Even if the person doesn't always act in ways that indicate that he is willing to be an ally, if you treat him as if he already is, it will increase the likelihood that he will become the ally you want.

We can break the cycle of mistreatment when we begin to treat people as if they're eager to be our allies. We do not have to wait until someone acts in a trustworthy manner. Sometimes by taking the first steps to offer trust, we can enable others to become worthy of our trust.

One helpful step in developing trust with a new ally is to tell that person what she can do or not do that will help you gain trust.

Notes

Identify at least one person from a different racial, ethnic, or religious background from work or school or your neighborhood whom you want as an ally. What is the person's name?

_____

What steps do you plan to take to strengthen your relationship with that person?

_____

_____

_____

_____

Principles in •
action

Birmingham, Alabama

In Birmingham, Alabama, as a result of the community alliances built through the Leadership for Diversity Initiative (LDI), the NCBI team was able to become a strong voice against the oppression of Gays, Lesbians, and Bisexuals.

NCBI Birmingham made an early commitment to include Gay, Lesbian, and Bisexual issues in all of its diversity training programs. In Alabama, where the Christian right exerts considerable power, even speaking about Gay issues in a public setting can be controversial.

Over the last five years, two Gay men, one Black and one White, became connected to the work of NCBI in Birmingham. They found that NCBI was committed to ending Gay, Lesbian, and Bisexual oppression, and they embraced the work of NCBI's local diversity training efforts. When NCBI Birmingham launched LDI, these two Gay men were part of the steering committee. They did outreach into the Gay community and worked hard to recruit one of the key leaders of a statewide Gay rights organization to participate in the ongoing work of the chapter.

After the initial LDI training, community leaders met for two years on a monthly basis. The monthly meetings often focused on examining the dynamics of the various forms of discrimination. In February of 1996, and again in March of 1997, the monthly meetings focused on Gay oppression. Not all members of the NCBI team were comfortable with supporting Gay issues. Some objected to the Gay rights agenda on religious grounds. The leaders of the team, including Gay members, decided not to vilify those who held this position. Instead, they tried to reach out to their neighbors by listening to the negative views about homosexuality that are common in the Bible Belt. After much struggling, the leadership team found a way to bridge the concerns of both groups. Everyone could agree-regardless of his or her personal views on sexual morality—that the mistreatment of Gay people was wrong and the oppression had to stop.

Since NCBI had a credible history with the Gay community, the head of one of the leading organizations for Gay rights in Alabama, who participated in LDI, telephoned Caryn Corenblum, the director of the NCBI chapter in Birmingham, to ask for help. The local Birmingham ABC affiliate refused to air the widely publicized television episode of "Ellen" when the leading character came out as a Lesbian. The Gay leader asked Caryn if she would be willing to organize a press conference of community leaders who opposed the television station's decision. Caryn agreed immediately to help. She contacted local organizations and community leaders and asked them to join her in denouncing the station's censorship as prejudicial to Gays, Lesbians, and Bisexuals in the community.

In the park near the Sixteenth Street Baptist Church, where demonstrations occurred during the Civil Rights Movement, Caryn Corenblum and Smith Williams, Associate Director of NCBI Birmingham, read the following statement to television and print journalists:

> *The decision not to show the April 30 episode of Ellen [by the local ABC affiliate] is the effect o f the ever-present oppression of gays, lesbians, [and] bisexuals. We . . . seize this opportunity to be seen and heard as visible allies for our gay, lesbian, and bisexual brothers and sisters. We are black, white, Jews, Gentiles, Christians, heterosexuals, gay, rich, poor, middle class, young, middle-aged, old, disabled and able-bodied. We as a community will not allow the scapegoating of one group. We know that ending racism, sexism, anti-Semitism, and all other oppressions will happen only*

when the oppression of all people ends ... We see the censorship of this "Ellen" episode as one more attempt to keep gays, lesbians and bisexuals invisible ... We live in a city whose struggles continue to make us conscious of the importance of freedom, justice and respect for all of its citizens. Inspired by the vision of ending the mistreatment of all human beings, we "come out" as allies against the oppression of our fellow human gays, lesbians and bisexuals.

The news conference aired again and again on local television. What began as an initial commitment by members of the NCBI team to be allies to the Gay community, developed, through the LDI project, to become a public showing of support that reached the entire Birmingham community.

Empowering

Leaders to Lead

Principle:
effective
leadership requires
individual *initiative.*

Theory:

Many people think that to uphold democratic principles within a group, all group efforts must require consensus. To adopt such a procedure is not only unwieldy, it inhibits individual leadership. For an activity to succeed, it requires one person to take charge and be accountable for it. Though there is a need for teamwork and consultation in any successful undertaking, the rhetoric of cooperative efforts often leaves no one in charge. As a result, so many times nothing gets done. It is far more effective to encourage people to take individual initiative. World events often move forward when one person decides to take a courageous step. Institutional change relies on the courage of individuals.

Example:

One NCBI chapter had tried for many years to build a base for anti-racism work in the city. For quite some time the chapter remained relatively unknown. When a new person became the director of the chapter, he was determined to have an impact on the city. He set up meetings with the mayor's office. He advised the mayor's assistant in planning a citywide day on racial reconciliation and healing. He then offered the services of the local NCBI chapter to facilitate the program. He put NCBI at the center of leading anti-racism work in the city. Why did it work? He took individual leadership. He decided the future of the city was in his hands. He built relationships with key civic and religious leaders. But most of all, he decided that he was not powerless, that he could offer what the city most needed.

Activity:

Taking leadership initiative requires a shift in attitude. You have to assume that you as an individual can take charge of the difficulties around you. You have to believe that you can make a difference. One person can effect change even when others are caught up in discouragement, powerlessness, or blame. When faced with a daunting task, ask yourself the following questions:

1. If I knew this project was completely up to me, what would I do now?
2. If I knew I was completely powerful, how would I act in this situation?
3. If I knew that everyone around me was eager and waiting for my input, how would I act?
4. If I truly believed my contributions could make a profound difference, what skills, knowledge, or insights would I offer?

We don't ever have to wait for someone to tap us on the shoulder and say, "Could you help us, or could you lead us?" Each one of us can make the decision to take individual initiative and move a situation forward. Deciding that you are in charge of every situation means that you have to confront the terrifying reality that you already possess the power to change the world.

Principle:

effective

leadership for diversity requires

having the integrity to take

principled **stands.**

Theory:

One of the benefits of a pluralistic society is that people with differing views can live harmoniously side by side. Sometimes, however, the social climate that favors pluralism can become disturbingly permissive. One of the distortions of pluralism is that even the most notorious behavior can become accepted under the rubric of tolerance. Yet, a call for standards raises other questions. In the rhetoric of current political debates, a call for standards has become a code word for a narrow political agenda, both on the right and on the left. The opposition to that agenda has often focused on relaxing standards rather than replacing them. What gets lost in the conversation is the need to have standards, to state what they are, and to fight for them. A common problem in current political discourse is that many of the most ardently defended standards are based either on the exploitation of people's fears or on comfortable, long-standing prejudices. The answer to this dilemma is not to ignore the need for correct policies and standards. We need leaders who are willing to speak out against oppression. We must expect that we, as well as other leaders, will face our own prejudices, so that our policies will be free of unchallenged presuppositions. Most significantly, we need to speak up, to state our positions without waiting to see what the majority thinks-to have the courage of our own convictions.

Example:

A member of the U.S. Congress from a tobacco-producing state cast a crucial vote on a budget measure that increased taxes on tobacco products. Many of his constituents regarded his vote as a betrayal of his district. The Congressman had grown up in his state, where his father had owned a tobacco farm. He was brokenhearted that the principled stand he had taken had been so misunderstood by voters in his district. Instead of retreating, he kept explaining the reasons for his vote. He also learned how to listen to the feelings of betrayal from his constituents. He found that he could listen without becoming defensive. Shortly after the budget vote, the Congressman participated in a televised town meeting in which elected officials responded to questions from the audience. His recent budget vote raised a great deal of concern. Without apology, the Congressman stated plainly the reasons for his vote; he was also able to articulate the feelings of betrayal that many constituents felt, and he was able to respond to their concerns while acknowledging how painful it was to be perceived as betraying the interests of his own state. Resisting the temptation to repackage his position to make it more palatable to the audience, his honesty and integrity won him many allies that night.

Activity:

Think of someone you know in a leadership position who took a principled stand. It may be especially useful to think of a leader with whom you disagreed but you nonetheless knew acted with integrity. What did that person do to earn your respect? What did that person teach you about integrity that you could use in your own life? What situation in your present life requires you to take a principled stand? What is getting in the way?

What the world needs are leaders who act with integrity, people who are willing to take a stand without waiting to see how popular they may be. Despite the most sophisticated reasons for gaining advantage by side-stepping the truth, honesty increases our ability to effect change.

Principle:

leaders

deserve to be cherished and supported while they are *leading.*

Theory:

We see all around us leaders who are not treated as human beings. First, they are pedestaled; then when they don't fulfill our expectations, they are trashed. Leaders are expected to be perfect. When they're not, they're brutally attacked, often in unrelenting public campaigns. On the one hand, we are in dire need of courageous people who want to take on leadership roles. But on the other hand, who is going to want to take leadership, if it might mean subjecting yourself, as well as your family, to constant criticism? Leaders deserve to be treated well while they're leading. We need to train leaders on how to muster support, on how to set up teams who can be counted on to back them under all conditions. It will be impossible to take leadership on the most difficult issues of oppression without a team of support. Otherwise, isolation and discouragement take over. Leaders deserve to be appreciated.

Example:

Two women in Northern Ireland built a courageous women's peace movement, rallying the support of both Roman Catholic and Protestant women in Northern Ireland. However, they faced constant criticism, not only from external sectarian partisans, but also from within, from the other women who were part of their movement. The barrage of criticism took its toll, particularly the criticism that came from other women. The women could no longer lead, and the women's peace movement folded.

Activity:

There are simple things to do that remind everyone that leaders deserve and can expect community support. At the end of every gathering, whether it's a committee meeting or a project task force, adopt the practice of giving each person a turn (1) to express a highlight from the meeting and (2) to say what in particular she appreciated about the leader of the meeting. Most of us have been trained to think that it is inappropriate to encourage or accept appreciations of our leadership. But it is important to train others to recognize the contributions we make as leaders. The simple practice of systematically appreciating leaders plays a key role in creating a climate that supports people in leadership. As a result, others are also encouraged to take on new leadership roles.

At work, many of us recognize that the most effective supervisors are ones who are able to praise the work of employees. However, we often forget to appreciate the work of our supervisors. We may be so afraid to be seen as fawning or flattering, that we forget that the person in a leadership position also benefits from our favorable comments. When was the last time you told a leader that you appreciated something she did? Leaders are able to do their best when they are appreciated for their efforts.

Principle:
attacks
on leaders are a form of
oppressive *behavior.*

Theory:

We recognize that people can be mistreated because of their race or sex or disability, but we fail to notice that people are often mistreated because they are in leadership positions. One of the most difficult problems for leaders is knowing how to handle effectively an attack. Some leadership attacks are direct. Someone may stand up and disrupt a meeting you are leading, saying that what you are doing is completely wrong. Other leadership attacks can be subtle, taking the form of "helpful suggestions" or whispered gossip which undermines your position as a leader. When you are attacked as a leader, it is helpful to remind yourself that you are always doing the very best you can, often under difficult circumstances. When you're leading a meeting and someone attacks you, it is important to remember that as a leader you have a right to lead. You also have the right to expect support for your leadership. Keeping this principle in mind, it is possible to anticipate the inevitable leadership challenge and to keep in reserve a strategy for dealing with it.

Knowing how to handle leadership attacks allows work to get done. When a leader is always permissive, listening to every negative comment, the negativity will bring the work to a halt. Alternatively, if a leader is rigidly authoritarian, unwilling to listen to any concerns, the ensuing rebellion will cause the work to be abandoned.

Example:

A man came to an NCBI training program, and it quickly became clear he had come to disrupt the meeting. He was hostile and kept interrupting the session with biting, critical comments. During the mid-morning break, I met with him. I said, "You seem really displeased with what we're doing. Help me understand what's going on for you." He then told me that his boss had sent him to this diversity training session because she thought he "needed help." He was understandably very angry. After I listened to him and agreed with him that it was wrong for his boss to send him to a training without giving him any choice, he began to relax and participate in the session. He ended up loving the program and subsequently sent many of his colleagues to NCBI trainings. He simply needed someone to take his concerns seriously.

—C.R.B.

Activity:

There tend to be two common situations that involve dealing with difficult people at meetings. The first and most common situation is that someone will make one or two barbed comments, expressing irritation at what was said or what happened in the group. Usually, the most useful response is to appreciate the comment and highlight some positive element in it.

For example, a person might say, "I'm tired of these stupid programs. This won't do anything to address the real issues out there."

Your response might be, "I'm really glad you brought that up. My guess is all of us here are trying to figure out what will be an effective way to deal with all these tough issues. Thank you for reminding us that we need to keep remembering how hard things are and not to settle for easy, comfortable solutions."

The key skill is not to get hooked into defending yourself or your program. You do not need to sell the program or convince the person that he will like what follows. If you can't find anything useful to say about the person's comments, you can always say, "I'm glad you said what's on your mind. It's important to me that people can be honest here, so thanks for speaking up." THEN MOVE ON. The mistake most leaders make is that they tend to get caught in a tug-of-war dialogue with a critical person. You have a meeting to lead, so lead. You can't stop to discuss every negative comment that someone wants to make. For most people, acknowledging the comment and finding something in it to appreciate is enough.

In the second situation, your positive words will not be enough. The person may have had a hard day. The person may have had a hard life. You may belong to a group that has mistreated his people. You may remind him of his least favorite aunt; or for whatever reason, he may just hate leaders. There are hundreds of reasons that prompt people to go at you while you're leading. You can't always stop to handle every difficult person. When the positive, acknowledging response is not sufficient, you need to adopt a different strategy. After the third criticism leveled at you in public, you might say, in as relaxed a tone as you can, "It's clear you're really concerned about what we're doing here. I'd like to understand more. We're going to be taking a break in about ten minutes. Let's you and I check in at that time." Then do take the break and do LISTEN to what the person is saying. In a one-on-one encounter, you won't be so much on the spot, with everyone watching to see how you respond. You'll be better able to use your listening skills to find out what's really bothering the person. You'll also be more likely to make an effective response.

In conducting hundreds of group meetings, we have learned to appoint an easily identified "empowerment person" at the beginning of every program. The empowerment person's job is to listen to complaints and to keep in close contact with the leader. The appointment of an empowerment person has many benefits. The leader is free to continue leading without becoming burdened by every negative comment. At the same time, participants have someone who will listen to their concerns. The empowerment person also acquires the invaluable skill of distinguishing between the legitimate issues that should be brought to the leader's attention and the personal upsets that need attention but have nothing to do with the present program.

Notes

Principle:

leaders

change more readily through generosity than through criticism.

Theory:

One of the major obstacles to supporting a leader arises when a leader acts in oppressive ways. What do you do when a leader is wrong, when she is not being fully effective, or when he acts out in an alarming way? Our tendency is either to correct the leader with harsh feedback or to abandon the leader, seeking leadership elsewhere. We must have a mechanism that allows us to cherish our leaders while we also challenge them to grow and face their difficulties with honesty and integrity. How can we do both at the same time? A process called self-estimation incorporates a balanced commitment to both caring and accountability. In doing work to eliminate discrimination, it is important to have a process that enables leaders to develop. Otherwise, we just reestablish the very oppressive institutions we are trying so hard to change.

Example.

Marilyn, a leader of a grassroots nonprofit organization in the Southern United States battled with feelings of being besieged and isolated. She had recently moved with her family into a mid-sized city to become the executive director of a community-based organization. The volunteers and associates in her organization saw Marilyn as self-reliant and extremely competent. They were amazed at what she was able to accomplish in such a short time. They also saw her as stand-offish, uninterested in their opinions. What they didn't know was that Marilyn felt completely unconnected to any of the people in the community. She was struggling on her own to raise enough money to sustain all the organization's programs. During the self-estimation process involving Marilyn and her volunteer staff, her colleagues were stunned to learn that she didn't think she had any friends. Many of them were convinced, observing her constant activity, that she had plenty of people in her life. If anything, they thought they were unneeded. As the volunteer staff realized that Marilyn's professional veneer hid tremendous loneliness, they made a commitment to get closer to her, to become her friend and ally. Their support allowed Marilyn to relax and become not only a more caring, but also a more approachable, executive director.

Activity:

A self-estimation can take place between any leader and the group that she leads. In a self-estimation, the leader customarily addresses the group first, answering the following questions:

1. What have I done well in my job as the leader of this group? Name the particular ways you have functioned well in your job.
2. What do I need to improve in my job as a leader? Name a number of specific areas that need improvement.

After the leader has addressed these questions, the members of the group are encouraged to speak next. (It is sometimes helpful to invite people to pair off first, giving each person a chance to think independently before convening as a group.) Depending on the size of the group, a certain number of people, usually seven or eight, are asked to answer the following questions:

1. How has this leader done a great job in leading this group?
2. Being as specific as possible, how would you like to see this leader improve?
3. How are you personally going to help the leader improve? This is the most important question.

The goal of self-estimation is not to put the leader out front for criticism and condemnation. The goal of self-estimation is to help leaders grow in an atmosphere imbued with the understanding that every leader is doing the best she can, given her strengths and struggles. Instead of simply giving "feedback" to a leader, group members must also figure out ways in which they can be better allies to the leader, thereby ensuring that the areas which do need attention can actually change for the better.

We can hold onto an accurate sense of our own power when we take creative steps to be an ally to a person in leadership. We need not resign ourselves to the victim role in dealing with another person's leadership struggle. When we want to change a leader, the first step is to figure out ways to be her ally.

HEALING INTO ACTION

Notes

Think about a particular leader in a group to which you belong. How has this leader done a great job in leading?

_____

_____

_____

_____

How would you like to see the leader improve?

_____

_____

_____

_____

What are you personally going to do to lend the leader a hand in working toward the improvement?

_____

_____

_____

_____

Principle:

a trusted

leader admits and corrects

mistakes.

Theory:

We see leaders all around us, whether they're elected officials, educators, corporate officers, or religious leaders, who either defend or cover up their mistakes. Often they blame others for their own wrongdoing. As important as it is for us to support leaders, it is equally important for leaders to have the courage to acknowledge their mistakes and then work to correct them. The ability to make an honest assessment and admit error is often the first step in establishing trust, especially in building relationships across group divisions. Defending one's own oppressive behavior or telling others that they're "too sensitive" or passing off every criticism as a leadership attack fails to create inclusive environments. Although leaders don't deserve to be raked over the coals every time they make an error, leaders must also be willing to admit their mistakes openly and to learn from them.

Example:

I was in South Africa the week that Nelson Mandela was released from prison. I had been invited to lead several NCBI workshops at a conference on "Building a New South Africa." The entire audience wept when the head of the White Dutch Reform church in South Africa stood before the group and explained how he had personally led the church down a wrong, immoral path during the years that the church defended apartheid based on Christian theology. He cried as he spoke about the ugly mistakes that the church made under his leadership. Acknowledging mistakes, however, can be hollow unless the admission leads to corrective actions. Yet, the courage to admit error openly is the healing first step in creating better intergroup relationships.

—C.R.B.

Activity:

This skill is a hard one for leaders to practice. Admitting mistakes may sometimes feel as though we are putting ourselves in a weakened position, when often the opposite is true. Practicing this skill with those who are closest to us can be the best way to begin. One couple actually scheduled a weekly time in their relationship to ask each other for forgiveness for any ways that they had hurt or mistreated the other during the previous week. Practicing this skill at home will make it easier to implement it with colleagues in a workplace setting. A regular check-in session could include the following elements:

1. Each person first states all the ways he has been thoughtful to the other in the past week.
2. Next, each person states all the ways she has been off in the relationship and asks for forgiveness.
3. Finally, each person has a chance to add any unmentioned ways he thinks the other person has been off, opening a discussion that allows the other to acknowledge the error and to seek forgiveness.

The advantage of instituting a weekly time like this one is that it prevents unspoken mistakes from piling up.

Being able to clear the air quickly and correct mistakes makes it much easier to build relationships between diverse groups. When people know that we are willing to admit and correct our own mistakes they are much more willing to accept our leadership and trust us with difficult decisions.

Principles in
action

Washington, District of Columbia

With the support of a leadership team, Larry Bell, the chapter director of NCBI Washington, was able to have a profound effect on improving the racial climate in the District of Columbia, culminating in leading a citywide Day of Dialogue, a day of racial reconciliation and healing for more than a thousand residents in the District.

During the initial five-day training program for community leaders, which was the first phase of the Leadership for Diversity Initiative (LDI), Larry asked for organizational consulting assistance involving the current position he held with a community religious organization.

As Larry recalls, one of the NCBI trainers told him, "You can lead!" Larry responded, "But I don't know what to do and where to go."

The trainer said, "That's not what's required for leadership-the first step is to believe that people will follow you. You don't have to have everything figured out. It's sufficient to notice that the current situation is not good enough and you want to do something to make it better."

Larry remembered, "Then [the trainer] gave me a phrase to try as a personal direction: `Follow me!' I then experimented by calling it out, `Follow me!' and people in the training cheered me on. I never saw myself as a leader anyone would follow. As a Black man, I had internalized all the negative messages I had about Black men leading. I was also reluctant to be a leader, because when I was younger, I did take leadership, and I ended up being abandoned. I would be left alone to face the brunt of any opposition, catching hell for whatever happened."

After the initial LDI training program, Larry began to attend the monthly chapter meetings of NCBI Washington. He said that what he learned from the meetings was that leaders did not have to be isolated. Learning how to support another person's leadership also taught him that when he took leadership of the chapter, he could expect and accept the support of others.

At the chapter meetings, people refined their training skills, organized community- and organization-based programs, and did healing work with each other. The healing work involved overcoming whatever personal obstacles got in the way of working against discrimination. Chapter members understood that at the heart of liberation work was the liberation of each person.

Following the kick-off of LDI, the NCBI Washington chapter decided to identify the person in the mayor's office who was responsible for diversity work in the community. Larry and his team scheduled an interview with the woman who was the director of the District's office for diversity. In setting up the meeting, Larry decided to put into practice what he had learned about supporting leaders. He decided to go to the meeting with no other agenda than to back the leadership of a woman whom the local government had already put in charge of diversity work. Larry let her know that she was already doing a great job, then he listened to her as she told him about her dreams for the community. Larry said, "I saw my job as thinking well about this woman who had such important work to do."

Larry also let the local official know about the diversity work that NCBI Washington had been doing. He told her that he and his team were ready to support her in whatever way she needed help. He said, "Consider us as a resource you can call on to create a more inclusive DC, where differences are valued."

When the city government decided to hold a community-wide Day of Dialogue to address racial tensions in the city, Larry and the NCBI team received an invitation to be on the convening committee. The committee included the leaders from various representative community organizations.

Larry decided it was crucial to gather a group of people who would support him in the work on the committee. So he chose a group of local NCBI team members to accompany him to the first meeting of the conveners. It quickly became apparent during the meeting how discouraged many local leaders were. Larry decided that his first step was to listen, and he paid careful attention to the despair in many of the voices on the committee. Larry noted that these were good people who worked tirelessly for the benefit of the community, but they had no place to go where anyone was willing to listen to their frustrations. The committee members noticed that Larry did listen, and they saw how well Larry's team supported not only each other, but also the leadership of the mayor's appointee.

Subsequently, committee members turned to Larry and asked him whether he thought there was anything they could do. Larry said, "That's when I stood up. I said I knew what we could do." He led them through a part of the NCBI Prejudice Reduction Model, which allows people to notice the wide range of diversity in any public meeting, to come to terms with the records of misinformation they have about each other, and to meet together as a caucus to express what they never again want others to say, think, or do about a particular group to which they belong. Larry said, "People still wanted to keep on meeting in caucuses, even after the committee meeting was over."

After Larry put forth his idea of what the group could do, it was as though everyone could breathe easier. They had a plan of what to do, and they had someone who was willing to do it.

After the first meeting of the convening committee, Larry and the NCBI team met to heal any barriers that kept them from taking leadership on the committee. To battle against his own feeling of insignificance, the team coached Larry to say, "Mr. Mayor, you need to get to know me-I am the leader of a powerful chapter in an influential international organization." Larry said that the most important part of the healing work was to keep focused on the truth: that he was a powerful man, that he did have the support of a team, and that he could have a profound effect on the racial climate in the District.

Based on their experience with Larry and the NCBI team, the committee of conveners and the mayor's office trusted Larry with leading and organizing the citywide Day of Dialogue, which was scheduled on the Martin Luther King, Jr. Holiday in the Washington Convention Center. Larry recruited and trained 40 local NCBI leaders to conduct the program.

Larry noted, "There were times I was scared. There were times I dropped the ball— I made mistakes and had to correct them. But with a team that understood what it meant for a leader to struggle, I was able to show my fears. I was able to admit my mistakes and still win their support.

"One of the learnings for me," Larry observed, "was that the more I showed where I needed help, the more I got the help I needed. Person after person in the chapter came up to me and said, `How can I help you with this project?' `How do you want things to go?' or `Can I help you?'"

The Day of Dialogue was a resounding success, a community-wide event that won national attention. The Day had significant follow-up. The conveners continued to meet and learn from each other. Building on their success, the committee planned a Youth Day of Dialogue, bringing together more than a thousand young people to take stock of the differences in the community, to notice what keeps people apart and what can be done to bring them together.

conclusion

We wrote this book for the many community leaders all over the world who are working hard to bring about social change. In the years of NCBI's practice, we have found that these are the principles that have allowed committed activists to become more effective leaders. We offer this book as a gift to all of our friends and allies who are devoting their lives to making a world that is right for

everyone.

Authors

Cherie R. Brown is the founder and executive director of the National Coalition Building Institute (NCBI). She has led hundreds of leadership training programs throughout the world for many organizations, including the U.S. Congress, the Public Broadcasting Service (PBS), the National League of Cities, the National Association for the Advancement of Colored People (NAACP), the Union of Hebrew Congregations, the Council on Foundations, the George Meany Center for Labor Studies, DuPont Corporation, Denny's Restaurants, the Los Angeles Police Department, Corymeela Reconciliation Center in Northern Ireland, and the University of Port Elizabeth in South Africa.

Ms. Brown launched pioneer intergroup work between Blacks and Jews on college campuses across the United States. She produced the acclaimed video, *Working It Out: Blacks and Jews on the College Campus;* and she wrote the study guide, *Face to Face: Black Jewish Campus Dialogues.* Dozens of colleges, universities, and secondary schools have institutionalized diversity training programs based on her models.

Ms. Brown has published numerous articles on intergroup topics and has been a frequent contributor to *Tikkun.* Some of her publications include *The Art o f Coalition Building: A Guide for Community Leaders, Healing Prejudicial Attitudes in Intergroup Conflicts: the NCBI Controversial Issue Process,* and *The Role o f the Community Leader in Conciliation.*

In addition to her work as the executive director of NCBI, Ms. Brown has been the leader of Jewish work in the Re-Evaluation Counseling Communities.

George J. Mazza is a federal civil rights attorney practicing in Washington, D.C. He developed with NCBI *Diversity and the Law,* a unique program that links legal training with diversity issues. Mr. Mazza has worked with numerous organizations, including Flagstar Corporation, the International Union of Bricklayers and Allied Craftworkers, the American Association of University Women, Allegheny College, and the Los Angeles Police Department.

Ms. Brown and Mr. Mazza have previously collaborated on the articles *Anti-Racism, Healing and Community Activism* and *Peer Training Strategies for Welcoming Diversity.*

Related Resources

Brown, C. R. (1984). *The art of coalition building: A guide for community leaders.* Forward by M. M. Cuomo. New York: American Jewish Committee.

Brown, C. R. (1987). *Face to face: Black Jewish campus dialogues.* New York: American Jewish Committee.

Brown, C. R. (1988). *Conflict resolution and prejudice reduction in the classroom.* [Available from NCBI, 1835 K Street, NW, Suite 715, Washington, DC 20006.]

Brown, C. R. (1989) Black-Jewish relations: A new vision. *Tikkun*, 4(4), 88-90.

Brown, C. R. (1991). The role of the community leader in conciliation. In C. A. Taylor (Ed.), *The challenge of change in South Africa* (pp. 29-38). Port Elizabeth, South Africa: University of Port Elizabeth.

Brown, C. R. (1991). The dynamics of anti-Semitism. *Tikkun*, 6 (2), 26-28.

Brown, C. R. (1992, May 18). NCBI helps cities face, resolve hard racial realities. *Nation's Cities Weekly*, pp. 6, 8.

Brown, C. R. (1992). Healing pain and building bridges. Interviewed by G. Hanlon. *Woman of Power, Summer*(22), 16-21.

Brown, C. R. (1993). *Sidwell Friends School diversity day keynote address.* [Available from NCBI, 1835 K Street, NW, Suite 715, Washington, DC 20 006.]

Brown, C. R. (1995). Beyond internalized anti-Semitism: Healing the collective scars of the past. *Tikkun*, 10(2), 440-46.

Brown, C. R. (1996). Four principles toward a politics of meaning. *Tikkun*, 11(4), 44-45.

Brown, C. R. (1996). Healing prejudicial attitudes in intergroup conflicts: The NCBI controversial issue process. *NIDR Forum, Fall* (31), 1-5.

Brown, C. R. & Herring, A. (1994). *Black-Jewish alliance building: Rosh Hashana talk.* [Available from NCBI, 1835 K Street, NW Suite 715, Washington, DC 20006.]

Brown, C. R. & Mazza, G. J. (1991). Peer training strategies for welcoming diversity. In J. Dalton (Ed.), *Racism on campus: Confronting racial bias through peer interventions* (pp. 39-51). San Francisco: Jossey-Bass.

Brown, C. R. & Mazza, G. J. (1996). Anti-racism, healing and community activism. *The Humanistic Psychologist*, 24(3), 391-402.

Jackson, E. (1992). Police brutality and the prejudice reduction model. *Law and Order*, 40(11), 77, 79-80.

Mazza, G. J. (1990) *Welcoming diversity in the workplace.* [Available from NCBI, 1835 K Street, NW, Suite 715, Washington, DC 20006.]

Njeri, I. (1993, April 25). The conquest of hate. *Los Angeles Times Magazine*, pp. 20, 22, 26, 46.

Rice, E (1996, May 13). Denny's changing its spots. *Fortune*, pp. 133-142.

Smith, D. C. (1989, October 23). Righting the wrongs of racism. *The Christian Science Monitor*, p. 14.

Order Form

Please send the following book:

Title	Price	Quantity	Total
Healing into Action	$19.95		
		DC residents add 5.75% Sales Tax	$
		Shipping & Handling	$
		TOTAL ENCLOSED	$

Name:

Address:

City: State: Zip:

Telephone: (   )

Shipping and Handling: Book Rate **$2.50** for the first book and **$1.00** for each additional book
(Please allow 3 to 4 weeks for delivery)

Payment: Please make checks payable to **NCBI** at **1120 Connecticut Avenue, N.W., Suite # 450, Washington, DC 20036**

For large quantity orders please call: **(202) 785-9400**

Order Form

Please send the following book:

Title	Price	Quantity	Total
Healing into Action	$19.95		
		DC residents add 5.75% Sales Tax	$
		Shipping & Handling	$
		TOTAL ENCLOSED	$

Name:

Address:

City: State: Zip:

Telephone: (   )

Shipping and Handling: Book Rate **$2.50** for the first book and **$1.00** for each additional book
(Please allow 3 to 4 weeks for delivery)

Payment: Please make checks payable to **NCBI** at **1120 Connecticut Avenue, N.W., Suite # 450, Washington, DC 20036**

For large quantity orders please call: **(202) 785-9400**